WANTING
to be
FREE

OTHER TITLES BY NEROLI DUFFY

Wanting to Be Born:
The Cry of the Soul

Journey through Cancer:
A Guide to Integrating Complementary and Spiritual Healing
with Conventional Treatment

The Practical Mystic:
Life Lessons from Conversations with Mrs. Booth

WITH MARILYN BARRICK

Wanting to Live:
Overcoming the Seduction of Suicide

WITH GENE AND WANDA VOSSELER

Soul Freedom:
The Life of a Spiritual Warrior

WANTING
to be
FREE

*A Spiritual Approach to
Addiction and Recovery*

Neroli Duffy

DARJEELING PRESS
Emigrant, Montana

To Daniel, for being the catalyst to start.
To Jenny, for providing the encouragement to finish.

WANTING TO BE FREE
A Spiritual Approach to Addiction and Recovery
by Neroli Duffy
Copyright © 2017 Darjeeling Press. All rights reserved

No part of this book may be reproduced by any means, including electronic, photographic or verbal recording, without prior written permission from the publisher, except by a reviewer who may quote brief passages in a review.
For information, contact
Darjeeling Press, PO Box 154, Emigrant, MT 59027 USA
www.darjeelingpress.com

ISBN: 978-1-937217-10-5 (softbound)
ISBN: 978-1-937217-11-2 (eBook)

Decrees from *Prayers, Meditations and Dynamic Decrees for Personal and World Transformation,* by Mark L. Prophet and Elizabeth Clare Prophet (1984, 2010), and some images used by kind permission of The Summit Lighthouse, 63 Summit Way, Gardiner, Montana 59030-9314
1-800-245-5445 • +1 406 848 9500
www.SummitLighthouse.org • tslinfo@TSL.org

Image of Kuan Yin: Wikimedia Commons / Rebecca Arnett / Tengu800

IMPORTANT NOTE

This book is intended to provide general spiritual insight and principles that can help in dealing with addiction. However, it is in no way a substitute for professional counseling or other forms of addiction treatment.

This book is sold without warranties of any kind, express or implied, and the author and publisher do not assume any legal liability or responsibility for acts taken or omissions made in reliance upon the contents of this book. No guarantee can be given that the practices described here will be effective in any particular case. If you are dealing with addiction, or if you are seeking to help someone else who is dealing with addiction, please seek help from an experienced addiction counselor or treatment center.

CONTENTS

INDEX OF PRAYERS AND MANTRAS

FOREWORD

I AM CONVINCED YOU CANNOT GET OVER ADDICTION WITHOUT God's help. You must realize that your reason for being here is to contribute to humanity and leave the world a better place for having lived here. Living a life for your own selfish aggrandizement is not only foolish but in the end also self-destructive.

I have seen this in my own life. Many years ago I had the house, the pool, the car and the high-profile lifestyle—but it did not make me happy. I came from England, where if you had a mink coat you had arrived. I had twelve mink coats, but there was never enough of what I wanted.

I did not know what on earth was wrong with me. I didn't drink huge amounts. But I felt like a deer in headlights where nothing was working in my life anymore. I could no longer function. When I finally got help and realized I was not alone, it all made sense. I was an alcoholic. I had a disease called alcoholism.

I went to my first AA meeting in an old raincoat. I went to my second meeting in a cold November in the United Kingdom in sunglasses and mink. I sometimes like to think I recovered in mink. In the end, all my mink coats were taken from me. Someone who helped me to move took them as payment. I found out later that he gave most of them to prostitutes! When I moaned about it at AA, I was told to "get over it." And I did. And there is little use for a mink coat in Houston, where I now live.

After more than thirty years in the recovery program, I no longer state that "I am an Alcoholic." I do not like that label. Like many of my fellow members, I say, "I am a grateful member of the fellowship." I serve whenever and wherever I have the opportunity. It is such a blessing. I go on missions to Africa. I serve at the local Krishna temple. I help other alcoholics and addicts in their recovery. I serve at my local church. Whatever they need, I do.

Now I tell other addicts, "You have a disease that will kill you if you don't do something. Giving it up may be the hardest thing that you ever do. But the gift of getting your life back and being comfortable in your own skin—possibly for the first time ever—is the pearl of great price. And to keep that pearl, you have to continually give yourself in service, and do it gladly."

I first met Neroli Duffy in the summer of 2013. I was visiting the headquarters of The Summit Lighthouse when one day I met a lady who introduced herself as one of the ministers. We began talking as if we were long-lost friends. As she told me about herself, she mentioned that she'd written several books. Her book about addiction was only half-finished because she needed more background to complete it.

We were an answer to each other's prayers. Neroli needed the information that I had, and I needed to share it with others. I had been in recovery for more than thirty years by then, acted as the Spiritual Director in two addiction treatment centers in the Houston area, and coached and counselled many patients in various stages of recovery. It had become my calling.

For the next three months, we talked about addiction and I shared as much as I could. It was, oddly, like magic between us, and I am very pleased to see that the book is now complete. It is such an important message for a world in which so many people are dealing with this problem.

In some way, we are all affected by addiction. Drugs and

alcohol are a shield that people use to cover up the aptly named "hole in the soul." And this affects not only those who are seeking escape, but everyone who loves them. Thus, the costs to society are enormous.

If you have reached the point in your life where the pain, misery and suffering of addiction have become unbearable, you have been given what some have called the gift of desperation. This book can show you the way towards a life that is far beyond your wildest dreams. If you are in recovery, this book can provide keys to strengthen you on your path to freedom.

There is a saying in Alcoholics Anonymous, "There is no easier way." But I believe that the spiritual techniques explained in this book, applied along with the AA recovery program, are actually an easier, gentler way. My hope is that all who are affected by the disease of addiction will find this simple book with its powerful message.

JENNY HUNTER

Acknowledgments

Many of the spiritual principles and techniques presented in this book are drawn from the lectures and writings of Elizabeth Clare Prophet. For more than thirty years she gave a spiritual perspective on addiction and the soul's desire to be free, and people from all over the world have found freedom from addiction by applying her teachings.

I am grateful to my friend Jenny Hunter for her invaluable input and feedback on the manuscript of this book and for generously sharing her expertise and experience as an addiction counselor.

And many thanks to Daniel for sharing his story with me.

NEROLI DUFFY

INTRODUCTION

A S A MEDICAL DOCTOR IN EARLIER YEARS, AND LATER as a minister and mediator, I have seen firsthand the devastating effects of addiction on addicts and all those around them. Addicts and their counselors will tell you, as they have told me, of the horrendous battle that addicts must undertake when they decide to climb back from the gates of hell to which their addictions have delivered them.

There are hundreds of books on the market with varying approaches to addiction—from 12-Step programs to mindfulness to approaches based on psychology. Many of these books have a lot to offer. But the purpose of this book is to go beyond those approaches and to explore the spiritual component of addiction. For there is a higher science of spirituality that can help to overcome addiction—a power that in most people lies dormant, for they have not been taught how to access it.

For some time, I contemplated exactly how I could write a book about overcoming addiction using spiritual keys and techniques. I did not want to write a theoretical book, but one that was practical and real. So I waited, feeling that God would give me clear signs as to what the book should be.

A number of seeming coincidences converged when I began to formulate some of the concepts for this book: a friend talked to me about a sister who was struggling with alcoholism; a fifteen-year-old boy came to me in tears after trying to get his thirteen-year-old brother away from drugs; a fellow counselor lost a son

1

to drugs and was concerned about the remaining members of her family; and finally the caretaker of a sixty-five-year-old told me about this man's addiction to pornography and how he had been too ashamed to seek help until a stroke rendered him no longer able to indulge his addiction.

All of these people were looking for a little book they could read and share with those they knew to help bring them back from the abyss. Some had overcome addictions themselves, and they wanted to give their loved ones the spiritual keys that they had used to overcome addiction. Nothing they could find in the bookstores met this need, perhaps because the book they were looking for had not yet been written.

Although I could feel this book pressing on my heart for some time, something was missing. I knew some of what I wanted to say, but I did not know how to pull all the elements together. And then I took a plane ride from Atlanta to Salt Lake City early one morning. That day, when I least expected it, God showed me the way.

The answer came through someone whose path gently but firmly collided with my own—a brief encounter between two strangers, yet long enough for an exchange of hearts, as strangers sometimes do. On that short flight, the outline of the book came clearly into my mind.

Part 1

Above the Clouds

A Tap on My Shoulder

IT WAS AT 34,000 FEET THAT I MET DANIEL, THE UNLIKELY fellow traveler who was able gave me the exact key that I needed.* I was on my way back from Brazil after conducting a three-day seminar-retreat for several hundred people on *The Way of the Christian Mystic*. The program had gone well, I had reconnected with some dear friends, and those who were there had shared a profound spiritual experience.

I had just come from an overnight flight from São Paulo, and I was pretty tired—a good kind of tired. I was in a reflective mood. As I took my seat, I curled up with a printed lecture on my lap, knowing that as soon as the plane took off I would be ready for sleep. The three-and-a-half-hour flight from Atlanta would be a good opportunity to nap before the final leg of the journey from Salt Lake City to Bozeman, Montana, followed by another hour by car from the airport to my home in the Paradise Valley.

I was seated next to the window with one seat between me and the aisle, and I was kind of hoping that no one would show up beside me so I could stretch out a little. The plane was filling up, and then a tall, well-built man about my age slid into the seat next to me. He was casually dressed and had a pleasant appearance—a fellow traveler on an early morning flight. He looked tired, too, and I thought I could sense that he was not really into talking. Neither was I. Perhaps, like me, he was hoping to get some sleep. We nodded, mumbled welcomes to one another, and tried to make ourselves as comfortable as possible in

---

* Names of individuals have been changed to protect their privacy.

those ever-shrinking airline seats. His legs hit the seat in front, but it did not stop him from almost immediately dozing off.

I can't remember at what point in the flight we started talking, but I know we were high above the clouds. The flight attendant brought coffee and something that resembled breakfast. The man next to me asked for a pillow but was told that there were none to be had. I smiled sympathetically and said, "You must be tired."

He smiled back and said that he wanted a pillow because he had not had much sleep, having been up most of the night after a training session in Atlanta. Then he looked over and asked me what I was reading. I told him it was a lecture about spirituality by Elizabeth Clare Prophet. Actually, its title was "Opposition," and it dealt with how to handle energy when things are not going well in your world. I spoke in generalities, thinking that an esoteric subject like this might be a bit more than my weary traveling companion would want to deal with so early in the morning. But if I am honest, in my mind he didn't look like someone who would be interested much in spirituality.

My neighbor immediately said, "I am a spiritual person, too. I have been for about four years, ever since I was humbled and had to get down on my knees. I kind of had a conversion experience when I was struggling with something and had to learn to handle opposition. God helped me, and now I feel free."

I was startled at his mention of "opposition," the very word I had avoided in describing what I was reading. I immediately thought, "Well, I shouldn't have judged this book by its cover." I flashed on how the angels had maneuvered to get us seated together, nudging us to speak to one another.

I knew an angel was tapping me on the shoulder, so I took a deep breath and told him cautiously, "That's interesting, because the title of the lecture I am reading is 'Opposition.'"

I was also thinking of my own struggle with breast cancer. It had also been a humbling down-on-your-knees experience for me. So I added, "A humbling experience will sure do it."

We swapped stories for a few minutes. I told him about my experience with breast cancer. And then he told me that his spiritual experience occurred when he was in the grips of an addiction that had plagued him for many years. He described the struggle and the fight to overcome what he could only describe as "the demons within."

When he did not say right away what kind of addiction he had, I knew that it must be something pretty personal. That did not concern me, because I had learned to take all addictions somewhat impersonally. I have found that although the names or types of addictions may be different and in human terms some might be more embarrassing than others, from a spiritual perspective all addictions are variations on the same theme.

All addictions have overwhelming desires and cravings that take over your life and enslave you.

All addictions promise fun and excitement initially, but they eventually lead the soul into the depths of despair and often to death, if not of the body then of the soul. If you are lucky, you find the strength and the help to get yourself out of the trap, but many don't.

Whatever it was that had plagued my traveling companion, I was glad that he had found a way out. I asked him, "Do you still have to struggle with the addiction every day, even though you are over it?"

"Every day," he said. "But it's worth the fight. I am a different person now."

And that was the beginning of a conversation that lasted the rest of the flight. I was wide awake now as we entered deeply into a discussion of his experiences with addiction. When we finally introduced ourselves, much later in the flight, it was almost as an afterthought.

Perhaps not knowing one another's names at first contributed to a feeling of anonymity that enabled a couple of strangers to talk so frankly. Perhaps he was able to be so honest because he knew I was a minister and formerly a medical doctor and he could trust my confidentiality. But I think there was more to it than this, because even from the beginning he did not hold back.

He told me that at the age of ten he had become addicted to pornography. His grandfather ran a hotel and had a small business on the side selling pornographic magazines and videos. Daniel delivered the magazines and videos to his grandfather's customers, and he and his little brother started to sample the merchandise in the paper bags before delivery. That was when they got hooked.

In the end, the addiction took over Daniel's life. He was spending hours each day looking at pornography in magazines, in videos and on the Internet. He had been married for many years and had several children who were now grown up and in their twenties, but his life had degenerated into a series of affairs and a numbing sense of despair. Sadly, two of his sons were dealing with the same addiction. He described the shame, the guilt and the hopelessness that accompany an addiction.

Daniel is a brave guy. He shared his soul with me. He was a businessman and a member of the Church of Latter Day Saints. Yet for years he managed to hide his addiction, even from those close to him. His wife and family had no idea of his problem until it somehow got exposed one day and he couldn't deny it any longer.

Daniel faced the problem in a remarkable way. He was totally honest with all of his family, from his grandparents to his wife and children, and he told them of his struggle. His wife stood by him, although he said that he would not have blamed her if she had left. He got professional counseling. But most importantly, he told me, he got spiritual help through prayer.

He felt that it was prayer that had really saved him.

Then he told me about a poem that he had written about his experience. He had shared it with a few friends, his family, and a stranger or two here and there, and he said he hoped to publish it some day. He asked me if would like to read it. "Sure," I said.

Daniel reached up into the overhead compartment for his briefcase and retrieved a photocopy of a handwritten piece of paper. Here is Daniel's poem, as I read it, high above the clouds.

Looking Back

I'm looking back and now I see
An ugly beast that was part of me.
He was my friend for many years.
He gave me comfort when there were fears.
He helped me through some troubled times.
A closer friend you'd never find.

For I was him and he was me,
We were as close as could ever be.
I didn't know him or think him there,
But he went with me everywhere.
He told me what to think and do,
"Buy this, go there!" It's part of you.
It's what you need, to make you feel
Love and comfort. You need the deal.

But soon I tired of his demanding ways.
He wanted more, he was wasting my days.
I had given him power long ago,
When I thought him a friend and not a foe.
But now I could see his ugly face—
I was his slave; I ran his race.

How could he be my own best friend—
And then betray me for days on end?
"I will quit, never again,"
This I cried, "Please, make it end."
Yet over and over, time and again,
His part of me would always win.

Now if you think you know his name,
Then chances are you've felt this pain.
And some, my friend, may think this fiction,
But he is real—he's called addiction.

Now looking back it's plain to see,
Addiction is the beast in me.
He's always there, he's made his space
Within my soul, and on my face.

Now that I see him and know him there,
I treat him with the greatest care.
His power still great—and yet so small
When I call on the One who created us all.
The Creator knows him and He knows me.
And it's through His power that I'm set free.

So if addiction is a part of you,
And you want it over, finished and through,
If you want to end the pain and strife,
Then go to the Source that gave you life.

Go to Him on bended knee,
And seek His power with humility.
Go to Him, both morning and night—
Without Him you can't win this fight.
Tell Him you need His strength and power
To overcome in weakened hour.

If your heart is willing, repentant and true,
This power of His He gives to you.
And now you have the power within
To start a new life and live again.

The Grip of the Beast

I WAS VERY MOVED AS I READ DANIEL'S POEM. I READ IT AGAIN, allowing the words to sink in. Daniel did not name the addiction he struggled with, but this did not matter, since his poem described the core of all addictions. Any addiction—whether it is gambling, alcohol, nicotine, drugs of any kind, sex, or any of the hundreds of different addictions that have been identified—is simply the biggest distraction from living a real life and from our relationship with God.

Daniel knew that people can be addicted to many things—food, sugar, outbursts of anger and so on. As one who had lived through it, he told me that he recognized the signs of addiction in many people he knew who were addicted to all kinds of things yet did not even know it. They were afraid or ashamed to admit it, even to themselves.

His poem eloquently described exactly what it was like to be in the grips of an addiction. I had seen this pattern in patients I knew as a doctor and later in those I had worked with as a minister. I had seen it in the lives of those who were in the clutches of habits—legal or illegal—that were hard to overcome.

I had even seen a glimpse of it whenever I struggled to overcome a habit that sabotaged my own life in some way. But more than that, Daniel graphically portrayed his struggle with the non-physical forces that were behind these problems—forces that I had only come to understand through the work of my teacher and spiritual mentor, Elizabeth Clare Prophet.

I could not help but admire Daniel as he described how

he had fought against these forces. He had true courage and humility, and yes, a deep spirituality. When I told him this, he told me an amazing story.

Daniel had been fasting and praying after his addiction had become known. One morning, as he was struggling and wrestling to overcome it, he had a frightening experience. He was lying in bed next to his wife, when he felt something grip the back of his neck—a firm and icy grip, tangible and chilling, yet not of this world. And then he heard the most awful sound—a growling, guttural moan that seemed to be from the pits of hell itself. It struck terror into him and frightened him almost out of his wits. He felt the depths of darkness gathering around him. And although he did not know the name of this being—was it Satan himself?—he knew that he was no match for whatever it was.

He got down on his knees beside his bed and prayed earnestly, asking Jesus to deliver him from the "beast" that was gripping him. Instantly the hand was withdrawn. A calm presence flowed through him and he felt at peace.

I looked into Daniel's eyes, and I knew that what he was describing was not a hallucination or an illusion. He was not someone who was given to exceptional experiences, and yet this was very real. He knew it and so did I.

We talked about angels, forces of light and darkness and what this malevolent presence might have been. I reminded him that Jesus had spoken of dark forces that are beyond our physical sight. He had told the apostles that some come out only "by prayer and fasting." Interestingly Daniel had been fasting and praying when this "thing" was removed from him.

I was able to describe to Daniel what I knew of these forces of darkness, how they acted and operated in people's lives to produce addictions. And he understood.

A Story That Needs to Be Told

I TOLD DANIEL THAT HIS STORY NEEDED TO BE TOLD. HE TOLD me that he wanted to tell it but did not know how to start. I asked him, "Well, how did you start the poem?"

"I got the middle two lines. 'Now looking back it's plain to see / Addiction is the beast in me.' And it just went from there."

I explained that writing a book can be like that. You can start anywhere, and it just grows. Maybe you get the end or the beginning or the middle first. Just start with what God gives you and go from there.

I asked Daniel if I could share his poem anonymously in a book that I was writing about overcoming addiction, and he said, "Sure." I also told him that he needed to write his own book and tell his own story in his own way. He was articulate and had the heart of a poet.

Daniel had fought an incredible fight, faced the worst part of himself and overcome it, described the process to a stranger in detail, and yet was not ashamed before God or man. He was even willing for me to use his real name in telling his story—in the small town where he lived, everyone knew anyway. But I advised him to think seriously and to pray about it, as such a decision could have impacts on his family and business as well as himself.

Listening to Daniel's story was profound. I shared with him what I knew of the forces of darkness which cause the "grip" of an addiction—and of the power of prayer and of the higher power that is greater than any addiction. I also spoke of calling to the angels and some other spiritual keys that could assist him in his continuing struggle. Daniel told me that what I shared was very helpful. I was happy to hear this, and I told him that he had also helped me. I believe that God put us together so we could help each other. I could explain what he needed to hear, and he was the sounding board that helped me to articulate what was on my heart, what I needed to share with others. Our three-hour meeting was the catalyst for this book.

Before we parted, Daniel and I reflected on how many others on our flight that day might be addicted to substances or other things. I said, "What if, after takeoff, the captain had asked over the PA system, 'How many of us on board today are in the grips of an addiction and wish that we could give it up?' If we knew that none of us would ever see each other again, I wonder how many hands would have been raised." We suspected quite a few.

It has been said that all of us are addicted to something. Addictions come in many forms: drugs of all kinds, alcohol, nicotine, gambling, food, sex, pornography, and even anger and other out-of-control emotional states.

It is sobering to think how many of us speak of freedom and think we are free, yet how few are free in the truest sense of the word. I believe that what I am about to share can be of benefit to everyone. In the following chapters I will sometimes refer specifically to drugs or alcohol, but the same general principles can be used for any addiction.

Whether we have an overt addiction or just a negative habit we can't seem to overcome, we can all learn from these principles and apply them in our own lives. Even if we don't have a problem with alcohol or cocaine, most of us have some area in our lives that we are not totally in control of, something we do that sometimes sabotages our highest hopes and aspirations. This is really part of the human condition.

The process of healing begins with the first step.

PART 2

RECOGNIZING ADDICTION

The First Step

THE STORY THAT DANIEL TOLD OF HIS RECOVERY FROM addiction is not unusual. He described a critical turning point where the light entered his being and displaced the darkness. But this was not an instantaneous healing. He still had to face the daily struggle to make the right choices that would bring about that healing.

But even this turning point was not the beginning of the process. Daniel's recovery began when he realized he had a problem and admitted this to himself. Recognizing the problem was the beginning of the solution.

Addiction counselors will tell you that most addicts are in denial. Daniel said that he knows people who have a problem with addiction who either do not know it or do not admit it.

A lot of addiction is hidden. Many people who are addicted to alcohol are able to control themselves in public. These "lace curtain drinkers" are gracious and social at a party. Then they go home, close the curtains and drink themselves into a stupor.

So how do you recognize a problem with addiction—in yourself or in someone else?

A Compulsive Need

THERE ARE ALWAYS CLUES THAT SURFACE WHEN ADDICTION starts to take hold. When the compulsion grows, it starts to become clear that something is taking over or controlling an individual's life.

Addictions take many forms. Chemical addictions include drugs, alcohol and tobacco. Recognized behavioral addictions include gambling, food, sex, pornography, video games, exercise, shopping, self-harm (cutting) and eating disorders.

Every person and every addiction is unique, but some common signs emerge. Any or all of these may appear with chemical addictions; behavioral addictions may have fewer overt signs.

- Activity: staying home all the time or staying out all hours
- Sleep patterns: insomnia, too little sleep or excessive sleep
- Energy levels: either low energy or hyperactivity, talking a little or a lot
- Physiological symptoms: cravings, appetite increase or decrease, diarrhea or constipation, trembling, hallucinations, sweating, coughing
- Appearance: unkempt, skin changes, looking different, tired, listless, haggard or haunted
- Weight: extreme loss of weight, loose clothes to hide this
- Associations: hanging out with a different crowd
- Interests: dropping hobbies or favorite activities
- Behaviors: secrecy, hiding things, stealing, erratic behavior, borrowing money

- Personality: threatening, unreliable, just not themselves, poor focus, depressed, a feeling of emptiness, frustration, bitterness or resentment
- Psychology: obsessions or paranoia
- Emotions: more volatile or angry, moodiness, bad temper or depression
- Problems at school or work

A clear sign of addiction is when the substance or behavior begins to interfere seriously with the positive things in a person's life. Addictions often cause problems in relationships, breakups with partners or domestic violence. They also commonly lead to problems with finances—not only as a result of money spent to feed a habit but also the inability to keep a job due to arriving late, leaving early, missing days of work, or poor performance due to lack of focus.

Those who are suffering from addiction will often take serious risks to feed their habit, such as going to unsafe areas to buy drugs, "borrowing" money from an employer, stealing, or trading sex for money or drugs. While under the influence an addict may also engage in other risky activities, such as unprotected sex or driving recklessly. Anorexics or bulimics can literally starve themselves to death.

Many addicts and alcoholics are also addicted to adrenaline itself. For them it is all about the thrill, and their primary addiction spins off other forms of addiction including pornography and sexual addiction.

The clinical definition of addiction is when a person engages in compulsive behavior in spite of the adverse consequences. Friends and family of an addict are often in despair when they see someone choose their addiction over all the good things in their life. "Can't they see what they are doing? Why are they making such bad choices?" Part of the reason is that the brain of an addict functions differently from a healthy brain.

Brain Development and Addiction

RESEARCHERS ARE NOW REALIZING THAT THE ADDICT IS physically and mentally different from other people. The way the brain functions in an addict is not the same as the way it functions in the average person. In fact, it is thought that the wiring of the addict's brain may be different even before becoming an addict.

Sometimes this is the result of trauma early in life, such as violence or emotional or sexual abuse in the household or the turmoil caused by a parent with an addiction. In other people, there may be no obvious cause. But whether there are pre-existing differences or not, addiction itself causes changes in the functioning of the brain.

If you began drinking at age 12, you are likely to stop developing emotionally at that point. When you quit, your emotional reactions will likely be those of a 12-year-old.

These changes in brain function are especially pronounced when people begin drug or alcohol use in the teenage years, a period when brain structures and personality are developing. This is one reason why tobacco companies target their advertising at teenagers and pre-teens. Ninety percent of people addicted to nicotine started smoking before the age of 18, 98% by the age of 26, so if you make it through your teenage years without smoking, it is unlikely you will take it up at a later age.

Addiction also affects personality development. For example, if you began drinking heavily or using drugs at the age of 12 (and

19

some begin much earlier than this), you are likely to stop developing emotionally at that point. So if you try to quit, you will probably find that your emotional reaction to challenging situations will be like that of a 12-year-old.

If your addiction started in the teenage years, you may find that you over-react to situations, you will be grandiose, you will blame everyone else for your problems and see yourself as a victim. You will probably not be able to take accountability for what is happening to you, because you are not emotionally mature. If you try to quit, you may find that the unruly emotions that begin at puberty will come up again. If you tried to escape these things in the teenage years through chemical means, you will need to work through them now.

Although the brain wiring is different, the good news is that the latest research in neuroscience is showing that the brain is much more adaptable than scientists previously thought. It may not be as easy later in life, but it is entirely possible to re-wire the brain to help overcome the patterns of addiction and to fill in the missing elements of emotional development.

The Path to Addiction

MANY ADDICTS AND ALCOHOLICS WILL TELL YOU THAT the first time they tried their substance of addiction, all their insecurities went away. It seemed to solve all their problems. This is a well-known phenomenon.

When you first start on the path to addiction, you are often delighted to feel that you can function better—or so you think. You have confidence where there was insecurity, friends where there were none. You can talk well if you were previously tongue-tied, tell jokes and entertain when you were silent, and you seem to be having more fun—even if you can't remember it all.

At a certain point you cross a line. What used to be an escape is no longer fun. Now you have to have that substance even to function. Then you start to become devious. You start to cover your tracks, trying to hide what you are doing from others—and perhaps not even admitting it to yourself.

If you could see your aura, your spiritual forcefield, at this stage, you would notice that instead of having light around you, it has become rather dark. And even if others don't know about your addiction and can't see your aura, they can sense that something is wrong and they start to become concerned.

Covering up your behavior is often part of the pattern of addiction. For once you take the substance into your body, something shifts inside. It varies on how long it takes, but eventually it is very common to see a different personality starting to emerge. Your children and your family are affected by your behavior, which adds to feelings of worthlessness. You may feel an incomprehensible demoralization.

You may even find yourself having to face the fact that you have done something horrendous while you were so "out of it," something that you would never normally do if you were in your right mind. But you are no longer in your right mind and have not been so for quite some time.

Something has taken over. The "beast" of addiction starts to emerge, and so does the not-self, or the enemy within—in esoteric terms the dweller-on-the-threshold. The not-self seemingly has the upper hand. You may feel like you could not stop, even if you wanted to. Or you may succeed in stopping for a while, but the anxiety and panic attacks ride back in. You are riding a roller-coaster and you are not sure how it is going to end.

To escape from the pain, you withdraw further from the world and go deeper into the seeming relief that addiction offers. But the escape is only fleeting, and all you see in the mirror is the pain inside. You may not even be able to look in the mirror anymore.

Towards the end of this downward spiral, there is often a desire to find a permanent release from the pain. Suicide starts to look like a good way out. Some never act on these thoughts, but many do—one in three people who commit suicide are under the influence of drugs or alcohol. Many more think about suicide or wish they could somehow just instantly end all the pain.

All of this because the more the substance is in your body, the more you engage in destructive behavior, the further and further you get disconnected from your Real Self and who you really are.

Some people go all the way to "hitting bottom" before they summon the will to reverse this downward spiral. Some people, tragically, never turn their lives around. But many do. The power is always there, within you, to reconnect with your Real Self and change the course of your life. But you have to claim it.

Facts about Addiction

THE WORLD DRUGS REPORT FOR 2012 SHOWED THAT 230 million people around the world—1 in 20 of the adult population—took illegal drugs in the previous year. The report also says that illegal drug users with serious problems, mainly those dependent on heroin and cocaine, numbered about 27 million, roughly 0.6% of the adult population. That's about 1 in every 200 people worldwide.

Tobacco and alcohol also have a huge impact on people throughout the world. Although illicit drug use was linked with about 250,000 deaths in 2004, alcohol claimed roughly 2.25 million lives globally during that same time period, while tobacco use led to an additional 5.1 million deaths.

The problem is much worse in America. The 2015 National Survey on Drug Use and Health estimated that 8.1% of the population over the age of 12 needed treatment for substance abuse in the previous year.

The cost is enormous, not just for the individuals whose lives are shattered or lost, but also for families and communities as well. In a real sense, addiction is a family disease because everyone in the family is affected.

Here are some more facts about addiction:

- The National Center on Addiction & Substance Abuse at Columbia University found that more than 80% of those incarcerated in adult and juvenile penal institutions were there directly or indirectly as a result of the disease of addiction.

- Drug overdose is the number one killer of offenders released from prison. Cocaine is the most common drug involved.
- Two-thirds of world's illegal drugs are consumed in America.
- Between 1995 and 2005 treatment admissions for dependence on prescription painkillers grew more than 300%.
- More than 29% of teens in treatment are dependent on some form of prescription medication, including tranquilizers, sedatives, or opiates.
- More than half of American adults have a close family member who has had a problem with alcoholism.
- In the United States approximately 1 in 4 children younger than 18 years old is exposed to alcohol abuse or dependence in the family.
- Parents' drug abuse often means chaotic, stress-filled homes and child abuse and neglect. Such conditions harm the well-being and development of children in the home and often set the stage for drug abuse in the next generation.
- Children with one or both parents dealing with addiction are at a significantly greater risk for mental illness or emotional problems such as depression or anxiety. There is also greater risk for these children to have physical health problems and learning disabilities, including difficulty with cognitive and verbal skills, conceptual reasoning and abstract thinking.
- Children of addicts or alcoholics are almost 3 times more likely to be verbally, physically, or sexually abused, and 4 times more likely to be neglected.
- Adults who abuse drugs often have problems thinking clearly, remembering, and paying attention. They often develop poor social behaviors as a result of their drug abuse, and their work performance and personal relationships suffer.
- In the United States alone more than 100,000 deaths each year are attributed to alcohol and drug abuse.
- One in 4 deaths in the U.S. can be attributed to alcohol,

tobacco, or illicit drug use.

- Among the nation's alcoholics and problem drinkers, as many as 4.5 million are adolescents.

- Adolescents are disproportionately involved in alcohol-related automobile accidents, which are the leading cause of death among Americans 15 to 24 years old.

- More than 75% of domestic violence victims report that their assailant had been drinking or using illicit drugs at the time of the incident.

- Adolescents who abuse drugs often act out, do poorly academically, and drop out of school. They are at risk of unplanned pregnancies, violence, and infectious diseases.

- It is estimated that 3% to 4% of the U.S. population have a gambling problem.

- Various studies have put pornography consumption rates at between 50% and 99% of men and between 30% and 86% of women.

- The Kinsey Institute survey found that 9% of pornography viewers said they had tried unsuccessfully to stop.

- Rates of young men reporting sexual problems have increased dramatically in the years since high-speed Internet has enabled easy access to graphic pornography. Thirty years ago less than 1% of young men reported experiencing such problems. Now the rate is as high as 35%.

- Many men seek help with their pornography addiction only after finding that it has resulted in them no longer being able to respond sexually to real women.

Facing the Problem

UNFORTUNATELY, ADDICTION IS NOT AN UNCOMMON experience. It seems that there are many people in the world who are living with addiction and running from the self. Many are fearful and do not know how to love themselves or how to be kind and caring towards their body, mind, emotions or spirit.

If you do not recognize a problem then it is hard to solve it. The first step in overcoming addiction is a level of honesty.

You may not choose the immediate course that Daniel took of being brutally honest with everyone in his life—not hiding anything. But most programs for addiction require that we look honestly at ourselves and state the facts before others:

Admit that we have a problem.

Admit that this is not who we want to be or who we really are.

Admit that we need help.

Long gone is any semblance of normalcy. You think the way you are living is the only way you can live now—shattered dreams, shattered lives, enslavement of all kinds. The anxiety level is huge. Panic attacks are rife. Who will I blame for my horrible life?

—JENNY

Many people never get past this step. They tell themselves that they enjoy what they are doing, that there is no harm in it, that they are in control of their lives, that they could stop any time.

To face the truth takes courage and humility.

Now What?

IF YOU OR A FAMILY MEMBER OR A FRIEND OR CO-WORKER IS in the grips of an addiction, remember that facing the problem is the first step.

The next step is to know that there is a way out. Know that what it says in the Bible is true—that there is nothing that is too hard for the Lord. The Lord helped Daniel overcome his addiction, and he can help you or your loved one, too. But it is going to take hard work—freedom is always bought with a price.

Be willing to work.

Be willing to change.

Be willing to be humbled.

Know that there is a higher power to draw upon.

Empty yourself and be willing to be filled with His spirit.

Be willing to receive help. Remember that no man is an island, sufficient unto himself.

Running on Empty

APROFOUND FEELING OF EMPTINESS IS A COMMON EXPE-
rience in addiction. There is something missing. Most
importantly, it is the sense of joy and wholeness in life.
On the next level, it could be said that all those who are engaged
in an addiction are really looking for love. On a spiritual level
they are looking for the love of God, which is in itself able to fill
all needs, to heal all wounds. Not
knowing how to find these things,
they try to fill that gaping hole with
drugs, alcohol or other temporary
highs.

Addiction is a problem with many
levels. There is an undeniable physical
component, which has to do with the
chemistry and wiring of the brain.
There are mental and emotional patterns that need to be healed. There is
also the spiritual component. The
most effective approach to finding
freedom from addiction works on all
of these levels, including the spiritual.

*Who is running my life
when I am running on
empty? My bank account
is overcharged and my
debt is overwhelming—
there is only unending
turmoil. O how I hate
living this way. I am out
of control—but I need
just one more drink
tonight to console my
fragmented nerves.*

—REFRAIN OF AN ADDICT

My friend Jenny Hunter, an addiction counselor in recovery
for over 30 years herself, explains: "Addiction is a soul sickness.
This is about your soul, and soul lessons are never easy. What are
you willing to do to live in this world at peace with yourself?"

Carl Jung wrote to Bill Wilson, the co-founder of Alcoholics

Anonymous (AA), about an alcoholic he was treating:

> His craving for alcohol was the equivalent on a low level
> of the spiritual thirst of our being for wholeness, ex-
> pressed in medieval language, the union with God....
>
> The only right and legitimate way to such an expe-
> rience is that it happens to you in reality and it can only
> happen to you when you walk on a path which leads you
> to a higher understanding....
>
> You see, "alcohol" in Latin is *spiritus,* and you use
> the same word for the highest religious experience as well
> as for the most depraving poison.

In AA they teach you that you have to admit you are
powerless and to call upon a Higher Power. This is a good first
step. But I would add that you also need to know that you *are* a
spiritual being and that God *in you* is greater than the guilt, the
shame, the fear, the doubt, the depression, the hopelessness and
everything else that comes with the package called "addiction."
All of this has to go.

There are many excellent books about the physical, mental
and emotional levels of overcoming addiction. My focus is on the
higher power within that can help you to overcome any addiction, no matter what it is. You can tap into that higher power
and let it recreate you as a "new creature in God." I believe that
this book will show you how to find this higher power for yourself. And if you have the courage to do so, you, too, can be free.

As a spiritual counselor, I have seen the profound benefits of
a spiritual approach to helping people overcome addictions. In
fact, many in AA say that they only found deliverance from
alcoholism when their spiritual life was in order. They look upon
AA as a recipe for treating the disease of alcoholism—but ultimately, the remedy is the spiritual path. AA and similar 12-Step
programs are one doorway to that path.

Addiction of any kind is a hell of our own making, and addicts are often very aware of the tormenting demons within. Spiritual principles make sense of what takes place in the body, mind and soul of the one who is addicted, and seemingly simple spiritual techniques can provide a much needed anchor and profound results.

So take up the kit of spiritual tools you will find here and get to work. If you are fortunate, you might find someone like Jenny who has been through it, who can take your hand and guide you on this path to spiritual freedom.

And if you find yourself alone—"all-one" with God—let angels walk beside you and lead you through the "valley of the shadow of death," all the way Home.

PART 3

THE SPIRITUAL DIMENSION

You are a Spiritual Being

And now you have the power within
To start a new life and live again.

LET'S START AT THE BEGINNING WITH ONE OF THE FIRST things Daniel said to me, for herein lies one of the most important keys to overcoming addiction. Daniel said, "I am a spiritual person." He knew this was true because he had felt the power of Spirit move in his life. We went on to speak of the power within, the Higher Self and the role it plays in overcoming addiction.

When Daniel said he was a spiritual person, he was right. And the same is true of everyone. The difference for Daniel was that he had contacted that power, while many others have not yet found out how to do this.

Jenny Hunter tells her clients, "Wake up! Your soul is seeking resolution and enlightenment. God did not create you to live this way. God didn't make any junk. You will find that if you are willing to do the work, your addiction, whatever it may be, is just a wakeup call, the impetus to get back to the divine."

The key to overcoming is to know who you are and who you are not—both what you are manifesting right now and your inner spiritual reality. Some of what you see may not be pretty. As Daniel described himself:

I'm looking back and now I see,
An ugly beast that was part of me.

Before we take a look at the beast that became a part of Daniel, let's look at who each of us really is—a spiritual anatomy lesson if you will.

Daniel, you, me—all of us—are mighty spiritual beings who happen to be wearing a physical body. Sometimes we forget this, and sadly many people are not even aware of this eternal truth.

At inner levels, you are a magnificent spiritual being. You have a Higher Self. It is above you right now. The angels see your Higher Self, and they know the reality of its existence. And you can know it too.

The knowledge that you have a Higher Self and a lesser self, and knowing when each is acting, is crucial to understanding addiction. When any of us lose the connection with our Higher Self, we can feel empty inside. Many addicts will tell you that the reason they drink and use drugs is to fill what feels like a hole in their own soul. The disconnection from the Higher Self is the root cause of this feeling.

Let's look at a diagram of you as a spiritual being.

The Chart of Your Divine Self

Your Higher Self

THE CHART OF YOUR DIVINE SELF ILLUSTRATES THE connection between you, a soul evolving on earth, and your Higher Self, which is shown as the upper figure in the Chart.

Your Higher Self is a great sun of light. It is actually the spiritual source that sustains your life, even the beating of your heart. The light of your Higher Self descends into your heart each day over the crystal cord connecting your Higher Self with your soul, which is shown as the lower figure in the Chart.

Your Higher Self is eternal.

Your Higher Self sees the big picture.

Your Higher Self wants you to be free.

Your Higher Self knows that better things are waiting for you, often just around the corner.

The power of light in your Higher Self is great enough to overcome any addiction, to heal any burden of the soul. Unfortunately, most people don't know how to consciously contact that light, so they miss out on the greatest spiritual asset they have.

Your Soul

YOUR SOUL IS REPRESENTED BY THE LOWER FIGURE IN THE Chart. But there is more to you than meets the eye. You know that you have a physical body through which you function on earth. Besides your physical body, you have three other bodies.

You have an etheric body, or memory body, where all of your past (from this and all your previous lifetimes) is recorded.

You have a mental body through which you think and study and learn. Your brain is part of the physical body which allows access to the functions of the mental body.

And you have an emotional or astral body through which you feel.

These three finer bodies, plus the physical, make up what are called your *four lower bodies*. These are four interpenetrating sheaths of consciousness that allow you to experience the world and fulfill your destiny.

The middle figure in the Chart is another aspect of your Higher Self. It is the individual presence of the Universal Christ, the mediator between the absolute Good of the upper figure in the Chart and the soul evolving in the world of relative good and evil.

The middle figure is often called the Christ Self, and we are most aware of that presence as the voice of conscience. The upper figure is also known as the I AM Presence—the individual portion of the great "I AM" that God is.

Emotions—*Energy in Motion*

A S WE WILL SEE IN MORE DETAIL LATER, ADDICTION IS INTI-
mately connected with the energy flow within the four
lower bodies and within the energy centers in the body.
It often expresses itself in strong emotions.

You can think of e-motion as simply *energy-in-motion.*
People caught up in addiction are often quite aware of the flow of
emotional energy in their worlds. Addicts and alcoholics are often
extremely sensitive—their emotions are more raw than those of
most people, but they can't seem to get control of them.

One tough young alcoholic said, "I can cause a fight in an
empty house!" The AA *Big Book* says, "If we were to live, we
had to be free of anger." But how to achieve this?

Many who suffer from anger do not know how to express or
release their emotions in an appropriate way. The anger comes
out in ways that are very destructive to the addict and those
around that one. Others may not be in touch with their anger.
They may cry a lot or wallow in self-pity or other emotional
displays. Their counselors will tell you that their anger is turned
inward. There may even be a surface depression or passivity that
masks the stream of anger running beneath.

Inability to deal with emotions often begins in childhood in
an environment with parents who themselves struggled with an
addiction and were unable to handle their own emotions. It may
begin with suppressing emotions in an attempt to maintain some
sense of control, and thereby safety, in an environment of chaos
or loss. Ironically, this often leads people down a path to out-

picturing the same chaos in their own lives.

Jenny recalls being raised in a household where love was never expressed and expression of any kind of emotion or affection was not tolerated. Even as a small child, if something went wrong she was simply told, "Go to your room." She says, "There was no discussion. It was always my punishment. I was never allowed to cry. So I would go to my room and smolder. But all that energy had to go somewhere, and it came out later in anger and in abuse of alcohol."

In order to master our emotions, we need to give ourselves the permission to be vulnerable and to feel our feelings instead of trying to suppress them or drown them out. This means that we need to be willing to feel our sadness, pain and anger—but when we are willing to do this, it also opens the door for us to feel love, joy and peace.

There is a monster hanging around us as addicts, and its name is anger. The predominant feeling for any addict is rage, which produces a toxic mind and a toxic liver. The anger says, "I am the king and you will obey me." These internal "kings" and "queens" are very dangerous—and as with all narcissists, it is all about them and their needs.

—JENNY

If we didn't learn how to do this in childhood, if we didn't have role models to show us how to do this or an environment that allowed it, we may need to learn this skill as adults. It takes work, but we can learn mastery of our minds and our emotions. And we do it through our seven energy centers.

Your Seven Energy Centers

WITHIN YOUR FOUR LOWER BODIES THERE ARE SEVEN primary energy centers, which are called *chakras*. A chakra is a sending and receiving station for spiritual energy. Your chakras also regulate the flow of God's energy to different parts of your body. If we want to understand addiction and how it works, we really need to understand the flow of energy in our bodies and our chakras.

The seven major chakras are positioned along the spinal column from the base of the spine to the crown. Each of the seven energy centers has a specific color, energy and vibration, and certain unique qualities. Each chakra is like a flower—it has a certain number of petals, increasing in number exponentially from the base-of-the-spine chakra, with four petals, to the top of the head, the crown chakra, sometimes referred to in the East as the thousand-petaled lotus.

As sending or receiving stations, our chakras are dynamic energy centers that constantly take in, send out and store spiritual light. They are continually changing and never static.

We can use the chakras correctly or we can misuse them. The correct care and use of these centers leads to greater vitality in our physical body as well as the three finer bodies. When we correctly use the energy of our chakras we have greater strength in our physical body, greater peace and a sense of calm in our emotional body, greater peace of mind and clarity in our mental body, and greater spiritual energy and attunement with the realms of light in our etheric body.

Beginning with the base of the spine, the seven chakras are as follows:

Base of the Spine

The base-of-the-spine chakra is white, and it has four petals. It is the center of purity, hope, joy and self-discipline. The base-of-the-spine chakra is the lowest point to which the white light of our energy force descends in our body. We are intended to raise the light of this chakra through all of the chakras for their nourishment. In fact, the base-of-the-spine chakra is foundational to the health of the body because the health and vitality of this chakra affects all of the other chakras.

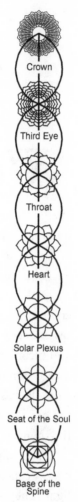

Here we experience the power of creation and the ability to procreate. Sexual energy is sacred—sacred energy in motion—and it is stored in the base-of-the-spine chakra, a powerhouse of light. We lose a lot of light when we misuse this chakra through inappropriate sexual activities or sexual addictions.

Many who are involved in addiction tend to misuse this chakra—whether through sexual favors to obtain the substances they crave or simply through loss of inhibition that these substances produce in their minds and bodies, allowing them to enter into alliances that they would never consider if they were in their right minds. Under the influence of drugs and alcohol, addicts often give away the very light that they need for their own healing.

Seat of the Soul

The color of the seat-of-the-soul chakra is violet, and it has six petals. It is the center for freedom, mercy, forgiveness, justice and alchemy. It is called the seat-of-the-soul chakra because it is where our soul is actually anchored in our body.

This is also the place where we get our "gut" feelings, or intuition. When we sense danger or that we need to leave or to go to a certain place or take a certain action, we often experience this "soul direction" at the seat-of-the-soul chakra.

Many who are in the grips of an addiction have ignored their soul's direction or intuition for quite some time. They have literally silenced the voice of the soul in the seat-of-the-soul chakra. Part of the process of recovery from addiction is learning to listen to the voice of the soul and the voice of the Higher Self, and then learning to be true to that "still, small voice" within.

Solar Plexus

The solar-plexus chakra is purple and gold, flecked with ruby, and it has ten petals. It is the center for peace, brotherhood and service. This spiritual center helps us to achieve balance in our lives. Located just above the navel, the solar plexus is the point where we experience emotions, both good and bad. When upset or angry or nervous, we usually feel it in the pit of the stomach.

All the uncontrolled emotions associated with addiction, including anger, rage and depression, are felt at the level of the solar plexus. Alcoholics Anonymous speaks of the process whereby "the dammed-up emotions of years break out of their confinement, and miraculously vanish as soon as they are exposed." When we are able to clear negative emotional patterns and gain a degree of peace and acceptance in our emotions through the solar-plexus chakra, we are on our way to overcoming addiction. Then this chakra can become what it is intended to be, a place of peace.

Heart

The heart chakra is our most important spiritual center. Its color is pink and it has twelve petals. It is the chakra of love, compassion and beauty, the place where the spark of the divine resides within us. All roads lead us back to the heart and the development of the heart chakra for greater love in our world.

If we examine addiction we almost always find an absence of true love and respect for others and for oneself. True love is selfless and cares for others. Due to the nature of the beast of addiction, addicts become self-absorbed and unconcerned for the welfare of others—and even less concerned for their own welfare.

Learning to love again is an important part of finding true healing from addiction, and it is often necessary to get beyond the negative emotions of the solar plexus in order to find the pure love of the heart. Jenny once described to me how she was able to do this by writing to each person in her life a letter that expressed her feelings towards them. In these letters she also said she no longer wanted to hold inside of her the anger and condemnation she had absorbed from them and she was returning that energy to them. Then she burned these letters. She had an intense mutual dislike with one of these people, and she was interested to see that the letter to this person would not burn right away and she had to make some effort to get it to catch alight.

This symbolic action helped her to let go of some of the negative emotional energy she had held inside. Then she found she was able to make the decision to love these people in spite of the past. Jenny says of her relationship with them now, "I let them all be who they are. I am gracious and loving to them no matter what they say or do to me. We are chalk and cheese, but love is the healing essence. Love is the secret weapon."

If we focus on true, selfless love—including love for our own soul—we can gain great strength from within and support from without to overcome our addictions. This kind of love takes courage, especially if it is something we have not experienced before. Jenny told me, "It is so scary to love and be who I am, who we are."

Throat

The throat chakra is the power center in our body. It is blue in color, with sixteen petals. It represents power, will, faith, protection and courage.

The throat is the chakra immediately above the heart, and it is closely linked with the chakra immediately below the heart, the solar plexus. Substances such as alcohol, prescription medications, and drugs of all kinds are taken in through the throat to mask raw emotions. Smoking of tobacco, marijuana and other drugs also involves the use of the throat and hence the misuse of the throat chakra. Negative emotions in the solar plexus are often expressed through the throat chakra.

The throat chakra governs the power of speech and the spoken Word, which give us the power to create, preserve and destroy. Our voice and our words can influence people for good or ill. As we speak to others, we can bless them or curse them, elevate or belittle them. We all need to watch our words and what we say. Better to be silent than to speak wounding words.

The throat center, like all of the chakras, needs to be purified as we recover from addiction. We can enlist this powerful spiritual center in helping us to overcome addiction in many ways, particularly in spoken prayer. We can also use our throat chakra to affirm the good in ourselves and others through kind words, an expression of appreciation or a positive comment.

Third Eye

The beautiful, emerald-green third-eye chakra has ninety-six petals and is located in the center of the brow. It is the focus of healing, truth, vision, abundance and constancy within us.

The third eye is where we concentrate. When we are focused on a problem or staring intently at someone or something, we often wrinkle our brow. When we visualize something or imagine something that might be, we are seeing it through what has been called the "mind's eye." Through this chakra we are intended to see God's creation, including ourselves, as he sees it—pure and perfect. Through the power of vision in this chakra we can then bring what we see into manifestation.

Many addicts have damage to the third-eye chakra that needs to be healed. Through rents or tears in their spiritual garments, the veil which normally separates the physical world from the unseen world is thinned, but instead of seeing heavenly scenes from the etheric plane, they can now see into the astral plane and are witness to many terrifying and awful sights.

This damage to the third-eye chakra is often caused by the use of drugs, especially hallucinogenic drugs, but may also be the result of other factors, such as emotional abuse, biochemical imbalance or a karmic condition.

Many addicts and alcoholics must sleep with the lights on in their rooms for fear of what they might see in the darkness. When they are going through withdrawal they often see terrifying things that others cannot see. What they see does not have an objective physical reality, but they *are* seeing things that exist on the lower levels of the astral plane, which are the origin of the concept of hell that is found in many of the world's religions. Fortunately there are spiritual techniques to heal and seal the third eye.

One sixteen-year-old boy told me that he could see so many unpleasant things through his third eye that life was extremely challenging. He had difficulty sleeping at night, and things that he simply did not want to see were interfering with his activities in the daytime. I encouraged him to pray for his third eye to once again be sealed, and his prayer was answered. To his great relief, he no longer saw the dark images of the astral plane.

Part of the ability to recover from addiction involves the use of the third eye through true divine vision. We need to be able to envision the possibility of recovery, to see ourselves as whole and free of addiction. If we can hold an image within our third eye of ourselves or a loved one as whole and healthy, free from their addiction, we can magnetize that state of wholeness to them. What we can see, we can manifest and become.

Crown

The golden-yellow crown chakra has 972 petals and is located at the top of the head. In the art of both East and West, the light emanations of this chakra are depicted symbolically as the halo of the saints. This chakra is the center for illumination, wisdom, self-knowledge and understanding. The crown chakra also relates to the mind and the thoughts.

The mind has a great deal of power. Some say that the disease of addiction is really an obsession of the mind. Addicts can be said to suffer from thought disorders—which might be anything from frantic madness to a sense of uselessness, loathing or self-pity. Some even say that all addicts are addicted to the mental process of suffering.

A number of drugs directly affect the crown chakra. For example, just as the tar and other components of tobacco deposit in the lungs, there is also an astral tobacco film spread over the crown chakra of those who smoke. This diminishes the flow of spiritual energy to the smoker, particularly the yellow-hued light of illumination necessary for enlightenment and spiritual attainment.

The full healing of these negative effects requires the clearing of residues from the physical brain as well as clearing and healing the mind and mental body and the energy centers in the finer bodies. This can be accelerated by a cleansing diet and fasting combined with the use of the violet flame (which we will discuss in Part 6).

When the brain and the crown chakra are clear, we can use the wisdom of the crown and of the higher mind itself to help us overcome the negative patterns of addiction in the mental body.

A Downward Spiral

ONE OF THE MOST HELPFUL THINGS I SHARED WITH Daniel was how addictions work when viewed from the spiritual realm. One element common to all addictions is that they involve a compulsive need. I believe that this compulsion can be most easily explained in terms of the energy flow within the spiritual centers and in the aura.

The base-of-the-spine center is intended to be the source of a fountain of spiritual light available to water all of the other chakras. If the energy can be raised each day from the base to the crown, as it flows along the spine it is then available to be expressed through all of the chakras in many forms, including greater awareness, love, feelings of joy and peace, spiritual insight, intuition, understanding, clear spiritual vision, and ability to master the challenges of life.

Every day, an allotment of energy descends from our Higher Self over the crystal cord into our spiritual centers. This means we only have so much energy available for our use each day. When we use it up, it is gone, and we have to wait for the next increment on the following day.

Any form of addiction will cause us to lose light in the spiritual centers. The energy or the light within us is literally the energy that feeds addiction. An addiction has no power over us except the power that we give it through misusing the light of the chakras.

In the case of Daniel's addiction to pornography, the loss of light would have been most noticeable in the third-eye chakra, through attention and visualization, and through the base-of-the-spine chakra, the center associated with misuses of sexual energy.

Other addictions may result in the loss of energy from other spiritual centers. For example, smoking centers on the throat chakra as well as affecting the physical brain and the chakras associated with it, the crown and the third eye.

Alcohol also involves taking in substance through the mouth and the throat center. Once alcohol is in the body, it can have effects on many of the other chakras. The physical substance of alcohol directly affects the brain, shutting down higher functions that have to do with the third eye and the crown. Unchecked by the higher mind, emotional energies of the solar plexus are often misused through anger or manipulation of others. The throat chakra may be misused

Every day, an allotment of energy descends from our Higher Self over the crystal cord, so we only have a certain amount of energy for our use each day. When we use it up, it is gone, and we have to wait for the next increment on the following day.

through angry words or lies. Long term alcohol abuse damages the liver (an organ associated with the solar plexus) and greatly increases the risk of throat cancer.

The use of other drugs often involves more than one of the spiritual centers. The throat chakra can be misused when the drug is ingested or inhaled. Drugs that have a hallucinogenic effect particularly affect the third-eye chakra, forcing the chakra open to see beyond the physical, and possibly causing tears in the delicate fabric of the chakra and the aura. The crown chakra becomes clouded over and poor judgment is reinforced.

Almost all addictions involve a misuse of the solar-plexus chakra through lack of emotional control. And substance like crack cocaine produces such an intense effect that it seems to result in a release of light from all the chakras at once.

This loss of light and the flow of energy that it entails is what creates the high of drugs or other addictive activities. In some ways this is like a synthetic spiritual experience. The difference is that in a true spiritual experience, what we feel is a flow of energy from our Higher Self entering into our four lower bodies, and there is a recharge and a net gain of light. In harmful habits, the flow is outward and there is a net loss.

After the initial release of light and the sensation of pleasure or euphoria this creates, there is less light in the chakras and the aura, a feeling of dullness, a let-down. (The hangover produced by alcohol is one example.) Whether the addiction is chemical or behavioral, there is a flatness to life, an inability to experience pleasure, which leads the addict to seek out the experience in order to feel the "high" again. And so the cycle repeats, each indulgence resulting in a loss of light, and each round requiring a stronger dose to have the same effect.

The end result is a loss of light in all of the spiritual centers as addiction takes over and every center is drained of its life essence. Victims of addiction can look as if the life-force has been literally been drained from them. They appear hollowed out and almost gray, even to the casual observer.

The tell-tale sign is often the eyes. These are intended to be the windows of the soul, a reflection of the inner light, but in the midst of addiction, instead of having light and vitality the eyes appear sunken or glazed and dull. We see this in the downfall of actors, models and rock stars in the gossip columns and the newspapers, and many of us have seen it in friends who have succumbed to addiction.

In the Grips of a Habit

A T A SUBCONSCIOUS LEVEL, ALL ADDICTIONS WORK TO-
gether. For example, people caught up in drugs often
have problems with alcohol or sex. This is not just a
matter of drugs or alcohol producing a loss of inhibition that
leads to sexual encounters. The addictions actually have a
synergistic effect, as loss of light in one chakra leads to problems
in others.

All addictions operate by enticing the soul to lose its light.
When the light is misused in the upper chakras, the light from the
base chakra does not rise. Energy then gathers around the lowest
chakra, which creates an uncomfortability for the soul. It must
find an outlet, which may lead to increasing sexual desires and
sexual activity that becomes more compulsive and unhealthy,
rather than based on love, and eventually more and more out of
control.

Over a long period of time, the loss of energy can have
serious negative consequences for the evolution of the soul. The
physical body is a temporary garment for the soul. At the end of
this life, the soul moves to other planes, and if on that day we
would enter the realms of heaven, the higher etheric octave, we
need a body of light, what is known in esoteric terms as the
"deathless solar body."

The parable of the wedding feast in the New Testament
illustrates this principle. In this story, the king invites the guests
to a wedding banquet. When he enters the hall, he says to one
of them, "Friend, how camest thou in without the wedding

garment?" The man was speechless, and he was removed from the feast.

The wedding feast is an allegory for the reunion of the soul with the Higher Self, the individual aspect of the consciousness of Christ. The wedding garment is the deathless solar body, the light body that is woven for us to wear in the heavenly realms. All of the saints of heaven wear this garment, and without this garment of light, we are not able to reunite with our Higher Self.

Each of us is supposed to be weaving our wedding garment a little each day, and it is woven from the light of the aura and the chakras as that energy is consciously used for worthy purposes, to bless God and man. At the end of our life, when we lay down our body and our soul takes flight into the next realm, we will want to have the body of light that will enable us to soar into higher octaves.

It takes time and energy to weave this garment. If we lose the energy from the aura through wrong choices, including addictions, then that energy is not available for the weaving of the deathless solar body. It is just that simple.

Addiction is a thief. While posing as a true friend, it robs us of the essential life essence we need to weave the wedding garment. Our attention is diverted to the addiction, which now becomes the object of our affections. Instead of adoration of the presence of God within us, our attention is placed on the flow of energy in a downward spiral.

The whole point of an addiction is to get you to lose your light. When the light is lost, it is no longer available for your use. Instead, the light is immediately stolen by the forces of darkness, which want that light and have encouraged you to spend it. These forces even laugh at you for your gullibility in listening to them. And although they are at fault for tempting you, they know that you had free will and it was your choice.

And who is the loser? Only you. You have lost your light.

You have lost your self-esteem. Often you have lost the financial abundance that has gone into feeding your habit. You may have lost your job. You may have lost family or friends. And you may well feel trapped by all of your wrong decisions.

Why is addiction so vicious? Why does the addict feel so trapped? Instead of weaving the wedding garment, addiction weaves coils of dark energy that wrap around the core of being. Each wrong choice wraps another strand of darkness around the center, until eventually it is so tight that there seems to be no way out—you are in a vise-like grip.

Your four lower bodies have formed a momentum.

Your desire body wants the substance or the object of the addiction.

Your mental body thinks about it all the time.

Your physical body has become hooked on this substance or sensation.

And each wrong choice carves a deeper groove in your etheric body, which begins to reflect all of the above.

In this state you begin to believe that you must have this to which you have become addicted. Your life is no longer your own.

> *He told me what to think and do,*
> *"Buy this, go there!" It's part of you.*
> *It's what you need to make you feel*
> *Love and comfort. You need the deal.*

Your spiritual and soul sensitivities diminish each day, until one day you can no longer hear the loving voice of your angels and your Higher Self. Their comfort and direction are replaced by the loud insistence of a habit or addiction that tells you that you need this and you must have it. As Daniel said in his poem:

> *How could he be my own best friend—*
> *And then betray me for days on end?*

"I will quit, never again,"
This I cried, "Please make it end."
Yet over and over, time and again,
His part of me would always win.

After a while the four lower bodies become accustomed to energy flowing in downward spirals. It even starts to feel natural or "normal."

The end result is often an early death, either through the effects of the addiction itself, or all too often at the individual's own hand through suicide—the result of depression or a sense of hopelessness when life has no goal other than to feed an addiction. Many an addict has come to the place where they have said, "I have to end this. I am getting out of this hell-hole for good by ending my life."

How do we get out of this web of darkness that we have woven?

As Daniel found, and as we explore later in the book, you can cut through the coils of darkness. You can clean up the dark energy, replace it with light, clear your aura, and heal your spiritual centers.

A major housecleaning is the first step, kicking out the uninvited guests who are messing with your mind and body, which are intended to be the habitation of the Spirit.

Stopping the Loss of Light

IF ADDICTION RESULTS IN THE LOSS OF LIGHT, THEN THE struggle to overcome addiction is all about stopping the loss of light and changing the flow of energy from a downward to an upward spiral, from negative energy to positive energy. If we heal the holes or rents in the aura through which the light is lost, we can gradually mend the aura and regain the light that we once knew.

Addiction is a slippery slope. It begins with one or two wrong choices, and then many more that compound upon one another. Addiction is the sum total of many daily choices that lead the soul downward. Many addictions build on one another. Once you take one mind-altering substance into your body, it becomes a lot easier to try another. Gambling and other behavioral addictions lead people to use alcohol or drugs to dull the pain.

The same process can be used to change course. Recovery begins with one right choice that leads to many right choices that reverse the wrong ones that took us down the dark road of addiction. The downward spiral can be turned around to become an upward spiral.

Louise Hay, author of *You Can Heal Your Life,* believes that "if we will do the mental work, almost anything can be healed." Her groundbreaking book looks at problems from a spiritual perspective. She explains that addiction represents "running from the self. Fear. Not knowing how to love the self." She offers an affirmation for those who would overcome addiction: "I now discover how wonderful I am. I choose to love and enjoy myself."

Addiction is a daily loss of light. We can begin the recovery process through any means that reverses this process and increases the light and energy in our body. It is a daily focus on right choices, first by not taking the drug or partaking of the addictive activity any more. From this point, healing can begin at all levels.

Those recovering from substance abuse can benefit greatly from clearing their bodies of toxic residues and restoring balance to all the systems in the body. The faulty mental patterns that are part of addiction can be reprogrammed, and emotional scars can be healed. And through all of this process, spiritual practice can be the driving force that propels more light through all of the four lower bodies.

PART 4

KARMA AND ADDICTION

Nature or Nurture?

IN DISCUSSING ADDICTION, PEOPLE OFTEN PONDER THE AGE-old question of nature versus nurture. They ask if addiction is a result of genetics or environment. In Daniel's case, his environment as a young boy had a lot to do with his addiction. Pornography was available, he started engaging in it, and a pattern was set that affected him for life.

If you are brought up in a household where drugs or alcohol are a part of life, the chances of your becoming hooked are also high. Studies show that children of alcoholics are four times more likely to have problems with alcohol. The likelihood is even higher in families where a parent is depressed or there is violence. So environment is a factor.

However, the risk remains elevated even in children who are adopted and raised apart from their birth parents, which seems to show that there is also a genetic component.

If you grew up in an environment of addiction, you may have to fight harder than others. You may have to change your environment to swim against the tide. But you can do it, especially if you invite the angels and masters to help you. Genes and environment do not represent your destiny. More than half of the children of alcoholic parents do not become alcoholics themselves.

But even more fundamental than these issues is the question as to why a particular soul is born in a certain family with a particular environment and a particular set of genes. And why do some people follow this programming and others do not?

Here we come to the often overlooked issue of karma.

Momentums from the Past

WE ALL COME INTO THIS WORLD WITH THE KARMA that we bring of our use and misuse of energy in previous embodiments.

I pondered this fact when I heard that Daniel had contacted the cause of his addiction so early in life. As I spoke with him on that plane, we touched on this subject. Daniel was not opposed to the possibility of reincarnation, but he had not thought about how it might apply to his own life.

I would not say that past-life karma is involved in every case of addiction, or even necessarily in Daniel's situation. But it is food for thought. If we take Daniel's life as an example for study, here is how it might work.

If we have lived before, the causes that we have set in motion in past lives can affect this life. Our thoughts, acts, words and deeds affected others. They were our energy, and we stamped our imprint on it as we sent it forth. This energy eventually returns according to a predetermined timetable for the cycling of karma. For children, karma usually does not descend before the age of twelve. But in Daniel's case, he was ten when he began to be hooked.

We know that we choose our life before we take embodiment. We choose our family and our circumstances, often for the precise purpose of balancing karma and for overcoming past momentums of negativity. We may have to meet the exact circumstances of karma where we created it in a previous life. If we were in the grips of an addiction in our last life, we may have to return to meet that addiction exactly where we left off—to overcome it once and for all.

If Daniel had been involved in his current addiction or a similar one in a past life, he might have wanted to embody into a situation where he could overcome it in this life. Maybe it was even a requirement of his soul pattern and divine plan that he do this.

Daniel had an opportunity earlier in his life to overcome his addiction. When he was engaged in his Mormon missionary service, he had been free from it, but when he returned to his old life, he also returned to his old ways.

Another possibility is that Daniel had in a past life been responsible for leading other people into addiction. Perhaps he was a pusher of pornography or some other habit, and he had influenced a number of people's lives for the worse. The debts to life that he owed to others eventually have to be paid by helping to free these people or others in similar circumstances from addiction.

He may also have been required to experience what it is like to be on the receiving end of what he had sent forth. It may have been necessary for him to struggle under the same burdens as those whom he helped to hook last time. In struggling with addiction this time around, he has the opportunity to balance his karma and overcome the negative force of addiction. He has fully tasted the cup, knows about addiction from every angle, and he is now able to help others who are dealing with the same challenge.

His family members may even be a part of a group with whom he had embodied before and with whom he must now work out a collective karma. Daniel was working hard to help his family members also get themselves out of the mire of addiction, and perhaps this was an important part of his mission in this life.

Karma and Free Will

HAVING SAID ALL OF THIS, IT IS IMPORTANT NOT TO FALL into the fatalistic concept of karma that is sometimes found in the East—that everything that happens to us is karma and that karma predestines our life. Karma does not determine our fate any more than genes or environment. New karma is being created each day as people make choices as to how they use their energy.

Daniel's exposure to pornography at an early age may have been his karma. However, it may have been that Daniel had no past karma with this addiction, that it was simply a matter of free will. His grandfather had free will to accept or reject pornography, and his choices affected Daniel and his brother. Daniel also had free will—and this is shown above all in his decision to overcome his addiction.

Karma is not predestination. Karma is simply the impersonal law of cause and effect—as you sow, so shall you reap. If we have sown unwisely in the past, whether in this life or a previous one, we will be required to reap what we have sent forth and to make it right, correcting the imbalance of energy.

There is also the element of grace. Daniel was given assistance to overcome and he had the good fortune or good karma of being raised in the Mormon Church, which gave him a spiritual framework to meet the challenge. He renewed his relationship with Jesus, and he had a support structure that helped him to fight.

Karma, free will, grace and opportunity are the great gifts that each of us has in life on this planet Earth.

Changing the Course of the River

RETURNING KARMA FROM OUR PAST LIVES, AN ADDICTION or a habit, the incorrect flow of energy in our spiritual centers—all of these are like a river that is no longer flowing to the sea but flows instead into a stagnant lake. In fact, the river has flowed this way for so long that it no longer knows any other way. Deep channels have formed in the rock and the sand. Off to the side, we see the old empty riverbed, now full of debris. How can we get the river back on course?

If we decide to change the course of the river, we must dam up the flow and redirect it back into the correct channel. The old riverbed will be full of dirt and silt and old leaves, and these must be flushed out. Then the river can flow in the way that God intended. It will take a little while, but it will flow again to the sea and be free.

It is indeed possible to change the course of the river. It is indeed possible to overcome addiction. It takes work, but the violet flame can greatly assist in flushing out the old riverbed and redirecting the flow of energy. This means a change in the flow of energy through the chakras.

PART 5

THE BEAST THAT IS NOT BENIGN

Entities

I'm looking back and now I see
An ugly beast that was part of me.

FOR ME, THE MOST FASCINATING PART OF DANIEL'S STORY was his experience with the "beast." This encounter was a key turning point, and it provides an insight into the area where the most important battle of addiction is fought and won.

What Daniel felt and heard was an intelligence that was not his own, a being that reinforced and embodied the addiction. In Christian or Buddhist terms, it would be called a ghost or a demon or an evil spirit. In spiritual or esoteric terminology, it is known as an entity.

Entities have been known throughout history. It is only relatively recently that their existence has been dismissed as superstition. People may indeed be superstitious about entities, but this is often simply due to a lack of understanding and not knowing how to deal with them.

The most common type of entity is known as a *discarnate* entity—simply a being without a body. Imagine someone who was addicted to drugs. When this person passes on, what happens? The desire will still be there. Instead of travelling to etheric planes of light (the heaven-world), this person may remain trapped as a disembodied spirit in the planes of his desire. In popular terminology, this would be called a *ghost* or *poltergeist*.

He will still have the craving for drugs, even though he is on the astral plane. He can't get them physically. But he can experience them vicariously through those who are in embodiment.

Those who have taken drugs roam the astral plane after they have passed on. They seek out those who are still in embodiment, influencing them to take drugs so they can feed off the light when it is released from their chakras. This is similar to how people vicariously experience sexual excitement through watching others engaged in sex. For entities, the experience is even more direct, since they can connect their auras to people in embodiment, feel what they are feeling and have access to their light.

The movie *Ghost* gives a vivid picture of discarnate entities. Sam, the hero of the film, has died. He sees many other people who have also died, including an angry ghost riding the subway. This entity has learned how to move physical objects even though he doesn't have a body. At one point, this discarnate sees a cigarette vending machine. He angrily breaks the glass and boxes of cigarettes fall out. He looks longingly at them and says, "Oh, I'd give anything for a drag!"

Addictions do not end at death. They carry over to the other side, just as positive momentums of love and light also continue when we lay down our physical form.

An entity may also be only the astral sheath of an individual who has died. A soul who has some light and devotion to higher things may be taken by the angels to the etheric octave in preparation for a subsequent embodiment. But if the soul does not have control over the emotional body, the astral sheath, or astral *ka,* can continue a separate existence, no longer under the conscious control of the soul and the Higher Self.

The astral shell may wander about disconnected from the soul and yet affecting others with an oppressive energy. When someone passes from the screen of life, we can call to the angels to come and bind and remove the astral sheath so that it cannot go out and create problems for others and karma for the soul.

"So Close, You Think It's You"

THERE ARE MANY DIFFERENT KINDS OF DISCARNATE entities, but they all have one thing in common—they want your light. They want to get you to release the light of your chakras by some involvement with what they are tempting you to do.

It is possible to be addicted to many things. We can be addicted to substances and also to behaviors, such as gambling, sex, anger or violence. All destructive habits and addictions have accompanying entities that attempt to invade the body and steal the life-force. They fuel the addiction, because this is the means by which they can access your light. From a spiritual perspective, a key reason why anything is addictive is because these negative forces *attach* themselves to us, attempting to influence our thoughts, feelings, desires and actions.

Entities attach themselves to individuals through the nervous system and at the points of the spiritual centers along the spine. The classic entry point is at the back of the neck, as Daniel described in his conscious encounter with the "beast." Entities may also attach themselves at the heel, a weak point where the nerves are exposed. (This is the real meaning of the term *Achilles' heel*—it is a point of vulnerability to entities.) Once they are attached to us, entities draw the light that is anchored in the nervous system and the chakras, feeding off it like blood-sucking insects or vampires. Sometimes they may remain attached to a person for a whole lifetime.

One alcoholic may have up to a thousand discarnate entities

hanging on to him, waiting for him to take a drink so that they can vicariously enjoy the experience through him. No wonder that the urge to take a drink can seem overwhelming.

As Daniel described in his poem, when we are under the influence of an entity, it becomes very close to us—so close that we think that the thoughts and desires of the entity are our own. It is true that sometimes we will have our own negative thoughts and desires, but even these can be very much amplified by entities.

Entities are ever-present in the world as we find it today. They roam the astral plane, just beyond the physical, and hang out in places of darkness and despair, around places where drugs and alcohol are used, around bars or places of gambling, prostitution or pornography. They cling to people. They can jump from one person to another. They whisper their temptations in the ear and the subconscious, seeking to entice unsuspecting souls.

All destructive habits and addictions have accompanying entities that attempt to invade the body and steal the life-force. They fuel the addiction, because this is the means by which they can access your light.

Entities also have their agents in embodiment—those who promote their wares. These can be those who maliciously push the products of soul destruction, or they may be those unwittingly distribute them (like Daniel, when he carried the pornographic products to his grandfather's clients).

The angels are very familiar with entities. They deal with them all the time. And they can deal with the entities that are afflicting you or a loved one. Invite the angels into your world and see how the dark ones flee. The apostle James says, "Resist the devil, and he will flee from you." And you may also call for those devils to be bound, like the tares among the wheat, by the legions of Archangel Michael.

Mass Entities

WHEN WE LOOK AT THE SCOPE OF ADDICTION ON A world-wide scale, we can see that there are enormous quantities of energy that are fed into these patterns of negativity. These forcefields of negative energy merge and coalesce as thought and feeling creations of man known as *mass entities*.

There are mass entities of war, anger, violence, greed, envy, and every negative force. There are also mass entities associated with habits and addictions. These entities include those of liquor, marijuana, tobacco, drugs, misuses of sex, gambling, and so on.

There are also entities of death and suicide. Their sole aim is to tempt unsuspecting souls to commit suicide as a final solution to their problems—"sweet death." Each year, thousands upon our planet exit from life by opening themselves to the despondent vibrations of the suicide entity.*

Souls under the influence of an entity—whether a discarnate entity or a mass entity—generally do not even know that the entity exists. But they feel the pull. It influences their thoughts and inserts an idea, a thoughtform, of the substance that they are addicted to.

Entities may be very seductive, they may be aggressive, or they may alternate between the two extremes. The influence of an entity can be felt as a magnetic pull, almost like an undertow in the ocean. Once you allow yourself to get caught in its grip, it can pull you into the depths before you even know it.

---

*Marilyn Barrick and I described the action of the suicide entity in detail in the book *Wanting to Live: Overcoming the Seduction of Suicide*.

Entities Work Together

WE HAVE SAID THAT ADDICTIONS WORK TOGETHER. One reason for this is that their entities work together. For example, the promotion of harmful drugs is aided not only by the entities of drugs but also by entities of suicide, which take the light-essence of their victims that is released in the process of suicide.

The first indulgence, the first drink, the first entering in, is the first step in the development of an addiction—the first in a series of steps that may ultimately lead toward the suicide of the soul. The suicide entities that come to seduce the youth have calculated their steps of suicide as the antithesis of the spiritual path.

We need to pray for the freeing of all people, especially our children and youth, from addictions. A soul like Daniel should never have had to face the problem of addiction to pornography at the age of ten. Sincere souls must be protected from being placed in the position of making such negative choices.

We must also pray for the removal of the entities which prey upon them. This involves the clearing of the discarnates of those who have recently passed on, who wander about attempting to make those who are in embodiment engage in addictions.

It also involves cutting people free from the influence of mass entities. You can use the spiritual techniques discussed in this book to perform this clearance work for yourself, your family or loved ones.

The Name of the Beast

REMEMBER THE BIBLE STORY WHERE JESUS MEETS THE Gadarene demoniac? The first thing Jesus did when he was asked to heal this man who was possessed by demons (the term used in the Bible for entities) was to ask a question. He said, "What is your name?"

The demons replied, "Our name is legion, for we are many."

That was true, because many demons infested this man, the cause of his insanity. The demons knew who and what they were, and they knew who Jesus was. They pleaded with Jesus not to send them away but to allow them to go into a herd of pigs that was nearby. So that is what Jesus did.

The Bible records that the man returned to his right mind and that the pigs then ran violently down a slope and were killed by drowning in the sea. Even the pigs did not want to suffer under the influence of these entities.

This is an unusual story, but it illustrates some important truths about entities. Entities can infest living beings. They can travel from one being to another. They can be removed through the power of the living Christ. And most importantly, Jesus asked for the name of the entity because he knew that this is the key to its vibration and to casting it out.

What Does an Entity Look Like?

MY GUESS IS THAT RIGHT ABOUT NOW YOU MIGHT BE wondering what entities look like.

Daniel heard and felt an entity of pornography addiction, but he never saw it.

Does an entity or a demon look like a little red devil with horns sitting on your shoulder? Probably not. But an entity might actually perch on your shoulder and whisper into your ear.

A discarnate entity might have a form very similar to the individual in his last embodiment—like the subway rider in the movie *Ghost*. However, the body of an entity is made of astral substance, which is less dense and more easily malleable than the physical. So discarnate entities may take on different forms.

Mass entities may appear in entirely nonhuman forms, often animal in nature—perhaps like dinosaurs or the various beasts described in the book of Revelation. They take on different shapes or forms, according to their function.

The makers of horror movies often tune into these forces on the astral plane and depict them vividly on the screen. In fact, the power of these films to shock comes partly from their resonance with the soul's subconscious awareness of these inner realities.

Let's look at a few entities involved in specific addictions.

Tobacco Entities

THE TOBACCO ENTITY, LIKE MANY ENTITIES, HAS MASCU-
line and feminine aspects. In general, the masculine aspect
of an entity has a repulsive or aggressive energy, while the
feminine is attractive or seductive. The masculine form of the
mass entity of tobacco is called *Nicolus*, the feminine is *Nicola*.

The tobacco entity, when seen with the inner sight, has the
appearance of a giant worm—the tobacco worm—which is very
similar in appearance to *Manduca sexta,* an insect that feeds on
tobacco crops in North America. The entity itself manifests as a
form that is the size of a man or woman. It coils around the body
of its victim, its mouth attaching over the head area and mouth
of the person who is using tobacco. It has a flabby, grayish
appearance on the astral plane.

You may have seen stories of people who are dying of lung
cancer and say, "I would rather die than quit smoking." This is
not the voice of the soul. It is really the entity saying through
them, "I would rather have my victim die than that I be deprived
of the light which I extract from his body each time he smokes."

The tobacco entity is virulent and vicious, even to the very
death of the individual. It is easy to see why such entities have
been described as "demons" in past eras.

This entity takes over the body of its victim, creating an
insatiable desire for cigarettes until a person is a habitual chain
smoker. It gradually eats away at the body, seeking to destroy it.
Why does the entity do this? It gets all of the light stored in the
cells of the body. Through this light it perpetuates its existence.

The cigarette user may be very happy in his slavery. He may even defend his right to be enslaved. This is because the entity interferes with the soul's sensitivity to truth, clouding the brain, coating the lungs with soot, preventing *prana*, the pure air of the Holy Spirit, from entering the bloodstream.

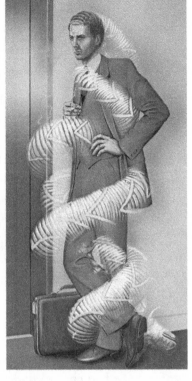

The tobacco entity has a focus in every cell of the body through the nicotine substance, through the smoke itself and its chemicals. The individual therefore, instead of holding light within his cells, is holding the consciousness of the tobacco entity.

Everyone who smokes has this entity and related discarnate entities in a greater or lesser measure. Their presence is known by the odor of smoke and by the general vibration. Those who smoke often have a certain similarity in their behavior—the way they hold their cigarettes, the way they congregate and the way that they talk. Even the gravelly tone of voice can be the substance making their throat raspy, but it can also be something more than that.

You can feel the presence of these entities in any place where people smoke. The presence of entities around these people does not mean that they are bad people. They are often wonderful people, but each one is a victim of the tobacco entity.

Alcohol Entities

ALCOHOL IS ONE OF THE MOST WIDELY ABUSED SUBSTANCES in the world today, and it has a very high addiction rate. The damage that alcohol causes to the organs of the physical body is well known, but beyond this, and even in small amounts, alcohol has significant negative effects spiritually.

Alcohol is a central nervous system depressant, which means that it gradually suppresses the functioning of the brain. The higher centers of the brain are the first to be affected—impairing judgment, memory, speech and movement.

These portions of the brain are also the anchor point in the physical body for the spiritual functioning of the upper chakras and the attunement of the soul with the Higher Self. One reason people make bad choices under the influence of alcohol is that they no longer have this contact with their Higher Self—which we most frequently recognize as the voice of conscience.

Without this connection, the negative elements of the sub-conscious are free to outplay, sometime causing great harm to the individual and family members. People often find them-selves unable to control their thoughts and feel a victim of them. Impaired judgment and discrimination may also lead to affairs, drunk driving and all sorts of risky behaviors.

Gradually there is a certain mental density that manifests around those who continue to abuse alcohol as the damage to the physical brain and the higher chakras, including the crown, builds over time and the connection to the Higher Self is weak-ened, even when alcohol is not present in the system.

Alcohol entities fix themselves to the chakras along the spinal column, often tying into the nervous system at the back of the neck. Through this attachment the entities pull out the light of the chakras, which results in the alcoholic feeling depressed after the initial euphoria of the light being released.

The mass entities associated with alcohol are *Spiritus* and *Spirita*, masculine and feminine entities which produce the combination of revulsion and attraction associated with alcohol. People often don't like the taste of alcohol when they first try it—a signal from the body that it is a poison—and a worldwide industry has been built with the aim of making alcohol palatable. The attraction of alcohol through entities, peer pressure, advertising, and the effects of alcohol itself leads people to become dependent upon something that they would otherwise shun.

There is a certain feeling you get when you walk into a bar. The reason for this is that the room is packed before the patrons even arrive.

These entities create in people the dependence on alcoholic beverages for relaxation, stimulation and euphoria. They destroy incentive and self-respect and wreck families. Millions of alcoholics and social drinkers are puppets to liquor entities and their previous victims on the astral plane.

Individuals who have been alcoholics, not having the light momentum to rise to spiritual levels when they die, hover around those in embodiment who partake of alcohol. As unbelievable as it sounds, there is actually a long chain of alcoholics in and out of embodiment who trade off lifetime after lifetime—some partaking of the alcohol physically, their companions partaking vicariously as entities attach to their chakras. Next lifetime they switch. These souls re-embody with the same desires for alcohol which they had in a previous life.

There is a certain feeling you get when you walk into a bar.

The reason for this is that the room is packed before the patrons even arrive. The discarnates are there, waiting for someone to come in and have a drink. They may attach themselves twenty-five or thirty at a time to the nerve centers of just one individual who takes a drink.

The alcohol in the body produces a chemical change whereby the light of the cells is released and becomes accessible to the entities. The more the individual puts alcohol into his body, the more light is thrown off and the more the entities can leech this energy. So the entities whisper in the ears of their victims, "Just one more drink, one for the road."

Marijuana Entities

MARIJUANA IS A DRUG WITH VERY DIFFERENT EFFECTS from alcohol, and this reflects not only the difference in the physical substance but also the character of the entity behind it.

In the short term, marijuana produces an intensification of sensory awareness and altered perceptions of time and space—leading some to what they believed were states of spiritual awareness. Hallucinations, anxiety and paranoia can ensue, more frequently with higher doses, but sometimes also at lower levels. The most widely seen effects of marijuana are apathy, dullness, lethargy and impairment of judgment, concentration and memory, which are well known as the characteristics of heavy users and present to lesser degrees in occasional users.

Alcohol is a water-soluble chemical that is removed from the body within a number of hours, which means that the immediate effects of the drug on personality are short-lived. It is well known that people often take on a completely different personality under the influence of alcohol. However, the next day they are more or less back to their usual self, maybe even with no memory of what they did under the influence of the drug.

The effect of marijuana is very different. The drug causes a short-term high as blood levels of THC spike. But because the active chemicals in marijuana are fat soluble, they accumulate in the fatty tissues of the body as well as in cell membranes throughout the body, and most importantly in the brain. Once there, these residues stay for a long time—for months or even years after using the drug. The effects of the drug on the function of brain cells and personality are therefore longer lasting and cumulative, and even an occasional user of the drug is always under its influence to some extent.

Another concern is the long-term damage the drug can do to the brain—especially for teenagers. A team of researchers from New Zealand found that those who had used marijuana on as few as three occasions before the age of 15 doubled their risk of developing schizophrenia by the age of 26. For those with a genetic predisposition to the disease, their risk increased ten times. And a long-term study in Australia found that between 75 and 80 percent of those involuntarily committed to a psychiatric institution had been heavy users of marijuana between the ages of 12 and 21. Just as with smoking tobacco and lung cancer, these effects of marijuana may not appear until years after use.

Marijuana particularly affects the physical brain, and this corresponds to the spiritual attack on the crown chakra and the third eye. The clouding of the brain with the substance of marijuana fills the cells with a substance on a physical level which has a corresponding effect spiritually—the cells can no longer contain the light of God. The damage to the third eye is reflected in the high rates of schizophrenia and other mental illnesses.

Instead of the bliss of union with God through Samadhi and meditation, there is the perversion of that bliss through the effects of the drug in the initial high, which is followed by depression or lethargy as the light no longer flows from the Higher Self. This results in a persistent poisoning of the centers of the brain necessary for the awareness of pleasure and the full awareness of being alive. The individual eventually has the experience of pleasure only when taking the drug, and over time higher doses are needed to achieve the same effect.

The marijuana entity itself has a gorilla-like appearance, at the same time presenting a seductive, innocent façade. A popular name for the drug is *Mary Jane.* In fact, it is an impostor of the Mother, the perversion of the Mother light, bringing a false comfort to her children, temporarily easing their burdens but in the long term cutting them off from their true self and causing great harm.

The apathy, lack of motivation, and loss of the sense of striving that are well-known effects of marijuana are the antithesis of what a soul requires to overcome karma and win the victory of a life's mission. So although it is often considered to be harmless, marijuana is known as the death drug—because it leads to the death of the soul and the soul's purpose in life.

> *The apathy, lack of motivation, and loss of the sense of striving that are well-known effects of marijuana are the antithesis of what a soul requires to overcome karma and win the victory of a life's mission.*

The concept of the harmlessness of marijuana is one of the effects of drug itself and the entities which perpetuate it. Their influence upon the population perpetuates the myth that it is harmless.

Marijuana users themselves often believe that the drug is harmless because they perceive no difficulties. One reason for this is that the deeper effects of the drug are gradual and cumulative, so people are not aware of changes from one day to the next. The very faculties of perception that would alert them to these problems are being damaged by the drug itself, and their ability to discern levels of their own God awareness gradually diminishes. Day by day they perceive no harm because marijuana is slowly destroying the senses of the soul.

The anonymous author of *Pot Smoking in America* provides a fascinating look at the marijuana entity:

> The pot smoker's unwillingness to stop smoking or
> even to acknowledge that he has begun to change are

caused in part by the entity. Drug counselors often report the signs of the marijuana entity, not even knowing that that's what they are discussing. "The scariest thing about marijuana to me is what it does to the kid emotionally—the culture and the identity they take on," says Steven G. Marckley, a drug counselor in Los Angeles. This "identity" assumes an inordinate importance in a person's life.

Marckley noticed that when people try to stop smoking marijuana they frequently experience an emotional trauma, a sense of loss like going through a divorce or having a child run away or losing a member of the family. "Over and over again the reality of 'I can't even smoke a joint once in a while'—the grief of losing that part of your life—haunts them. For a lot of kids, marijuana—drugs in general, but mainly marijuana—becomes their best friend."

A high school junior in Palo Alto once described the influence of the marijuana entity as "the pressure of the drug"—something not related to peer pressure—which gave her a hard-to-define, unearthly compulsion to smoke dope when she really didn't want to.

If you make the effort, you can quickly collect hundreds of stories from people who did not want to smoke dope yet somehow found themselves, for no logical reason, getting stoned.

Sex Entities

M ISUSE OF SEXUAL ENERGIES IS COMMON AMONGST addicts of all kinds, and there is growing awareness of the problem of sexual addictions. Addiction to pornography in particular is becoming very widespread with the easy availability of pornography on the Internet. These addictions are exacerbated by entities which amplify the sensation of sex and encourage the addict to indulge in sexual practices that cause them to lose their light.

Sexual entities can take on very seductive forms, even of physically attractive or sensual men and women. There are many stories of the saints of East and West being visited by such entities, attempting to seduce them. Saint Augustine and Gautama Buddha were both visited by visions of beautiful maidens who tried to lure them away from their spiritual path.

Most of us don't have our spiritual sight opened to be able to see these entities, but we can be equally subject to their influence. Daniel felt the presence of a beast, and he was no doubt visited by many entities of lust and sex and sexual fantasy. The names of some of the mass entities associated with misuse of sex are *Sensua*, the sex entity; *Voluptia*, the lust entity; *Masturba*, the masturbation entity. These are all feminine in nature. There are also entities of sensuality, self-love and self-infatuation.

Two other types of sex entities are known collectively as *Incubus* and *Succubus*. An incubus is an evil spirit in masculine form that attempts to lie upon persons in their sleep, and especially to have sexual intercourse with women by night. A succubus is an entity that assumes a female form to have sexual intercourse with men in their sleep.

These demons may assume the mask and the persona of individuals you know or have known in the past. You think you are dreaming of this person and are having a sexual experience with him or her in your dream, when it is actually a discarnate or entity that is trying to impose itself upon your aura while you are asleep.

The earliest accounts of these spirits date back thousands of years. Their existence became well known through the dream state, when the doorway between the subconscious and conscious minds—and between the astral and the physical planes—is somewhat open. However, similar entities are just as active at the subconscious level while people are awake, injecting thoughts of sex into the mind and leading their victims into pornography, promiscuity and all kinds of misuses of the light of the base-of-the-spine chakra.

These entities, like the seductive maidens who tempted the saints or the sirens who tempted Odysseus, often come in the guise of beauty and with the promise of bliss. When their true nature is revealed, we find that they are very virulent—like the beast that Daniel felt. Their goal is to suck the light of the chakras and leave the individual feeling debased and depleted.

Forces of Evil

ONE CLASSIC CHRISTIAN WORK WITH AN INTERESTING insight into the unseen forces behind addiction is *The Screwtape Letters,* by C. S. Lewis. The book is a collection of "letters" from one devil to a lesser devil, who is being trained in how to influence people in negative ways. The book is quite amusing in its description of the antics of these beings and how they lure people into indulgences of various kinds. Reading the book also reminds us that thoughts that seem to arise from within may be projections from minds other than our own.

Lewis was professor of Medieval and Renaissance literature at Cambridge University, and he also gained a keen insight into the workings of the unseen world. He understood that just as there is hierarchy and organization among the angels, there is also a hierarchy of beings of darkness. He shares some thoughts about them in his preface to *The Screwtape Letters:*

> Now, if by "the Devil" you mean a power opposite to God and, like God, self-existent from all eternity, the answer is certainly No. There is no uncreated being except God. God has no opposite. No being could attain a "perfect badness" opposite to the perfect goodness of God; for when you have taken away every kind of good thing (intelligence, will, memory, energy, and existence itself) there would be none of him left.
>
> The proper question is whether I believe in devils. I do, that is to say, I believe in angels, and I believe that

some of these, by the abuse of free will, have become enemies to God and, as a corollary, to us. These we may call devils. They do not differ in nature from good angels, but their nature is depraved. *Devil* is the opposite of *angel* only as Bad Man is the opposite of Good Man. Satan, the leader or dictator of devils, is the opposite, not of God, but of Michael.

Many of the spirits roaming about the earth are simply discarnates, people without bodies, and their consciousness while out of the body may be no different to what it was while they were in a body—simply seeking to perpetuate their existence and pursue their own pleasures. However, there are also spirits such as Lewis describes, angels who have fallen and are part of a hierarchy of darkness.

These fallen angels, like those Lewis cleverly portrays, do seek to influence those in embodiment. They also use other entities as witting and unwitting tools to accomplish their own evil ends. He describes the thought process and modus operandi of an evolution of darkness, whose outlook on existence is entirely different to our own. These beings are opposed to Life itself—the word *evil* is *live* spelled backwards. The word *evil* can also be thought of as *energy veil,* the veil of darkness that the devils (those who have *deified evil*) have spread over the earth.

The devils pervert the flame of life. They steal the essence and joy of life from their victims and use this energy to further their own goals. They include in their ranks those who have sought to acquire power over others through the practice of black magic. Black magicians and fallen angels can exist in the physical plane wearing physical bodies like you or I wear. They can also exist on the astral plane without a physical body.

When they reach a certain stage of adeptship on what is termed the left-handed path, they seem to stay in the astral plane more than the physical, sometimes for thousands of years. They can do more for the darkness from the astral plane by working unseen through people on earth than they could while working within the limitations of a physical body.

One might think that the beast that visited Daniel was a bit higher up the scale than your average entity of addiction. And this would be consistent with a habit that had spanned more than three decades. Forces of darkness do feed off the light of their victims, and they can become very entrenched.

The concept of demon possession is an ancient one and yet all too familiar even in this day. Family or friends of an alcoholic will often tell you that the person has a completely different personality under the influence of the drug. They see clearly when a force or entity is working through their son or daughter or husband or wife.

They see it in the eyes, the face, the tone of voice, the behavior—all entirely different from the person they knew. Even though they do not have a name for what they see, they know it is no longer their loved one who is controlling that body.

Understanding what is happening is a first step in the spiritual work to deal with these forces of darkness. Entities of addiction manipulate and twist the mind and the feelings of their victims. They loom large, but in fact they are very small when compared to the power of the Creator. Daniel's poem described it well:

> *He's always there, he's made his space,*
> *Within my soul, and on my face.*
> *Now that I see him and know him there,*
> *I treat him with a different care.*
> *His power still great and yet so small,*
> *When I call on the One who created us all.*

We will explore how to deal with these forces of darkness in Part 6.

Feeding the Beast

EVERY TIME WE ALLOW AN ENTITY TO TAKE OUR LIGHT, WE are feeding the beast. Like spiritual vampires, entities use our life-force to perpetuate themselves. They take in the light released, and they are empowered to entice others to also enter into an addiction.

Psychologists and experts will tell you that some addictions seem to behave as if they are contagious. They do not have words to describe entity possession, but they note a phenomenon which seems to be more than simply social pressure and the influence of environment.

Suicide clusters and copycat suicides are another example of a contagion that is fueled by entities. Those who commit suicide under the influence of suicide entities wander about on the low astral plane for a time until they must re-embody. (Usually they embody fairly quickly.) The astral sheath, being close to earth and earthbound, is a weight of oppression and depression that can influence friends or other members of the family to also commit suicide. The entities of suicide prey upon the next person and the next person and the next.

The cycle of addiction spreads in the same way. It is well known that addictions tend to run in families, and understanding the effects of entities we can see that this is more than simply heredity and environment. It is also stating the obvious to say that people who hang out in bars and with drug users are more likely themselves to become addicted, but again, this is more than just peer pressure.

The Lesser Self

AT THIS POINT IT IS IMPORTANT TO MENTION THE CRUCIAL role of the lesser self in addiction. The lesser self consists of the negative elements of the subconscious and the unconscious mind, the momentums of darkness that often wait for us from our past lives.

It is the lesser self that gets depressed, says the unkind words and does the unworthy acts. It is not real in the ultimate sense, in that it has no permanent reality in God, but it can seem very real at times, and its effects in our world are certainly far reaching.

The lesser self is our point of vulnerability to the influence of entities. The existence of this lesser self is what enables an entity to make us think that it is our own self thinking and acting, since there is a part of our own consciousness that vibrates in sympathy with what it is projecting.

On one level, the battle is external—an angel on one shoulder urging us to go one way, a devil on the other, also whispering in our ear, urging us to take the left-hand path. But the enemy is not just the Devil, the entity. It is the entity in league with the lesser self. The forces of darkness are external, but they are also within us.

When we understand this connection, we have another key to overcoming, and we can begin to outsmart the lesser self and the entity. Because just as we have a lesser self, we also have a Higher Self, ever-present, and it is often simply a matter of where we put our attention.

The lesser self knows that one day it will die—whereas the

Higher Self is eternal. When you finally have your victory, when you unite with that Higher Self and return to heaven, nevermore to go out, then the lesser self will be no more.

The ultimate goal of life is for each of us to become one with our Higher Self. A life that is centered on the lower self and all of its desires can make no progress for the soul. Serving others is the way to oneness with our Higher Self—for that is the nature of our Higher Self. In giving to others we find out who we really are.

Daniel saw that clearly. When he overcame his addiction, he was able to love in a way that he never could before. Free of the addiction and the lusts that went with it, he understood the true meaning of loving his wife, a depth of love that had previously eluded him.

Daniel told me that keeping on top of his addiction was a fight every day. Wrestling with the lesser self and one's inner and outer demons is not easy. But the rewards are great—sometimes beyond calculation. It is a battle, and like anything worthwhile, it takes effort. And like Jesus, who faced his spiritual battle in the garden of Gethsemane, Daniel did have to sweat, as it were, "great drops of blood." It took striving and effort. But he was not alone.

Who will win—the lesser self and the Higher Self? This is the point where the individual chooses good or evil, life or death, light or anti-light.

PART 6

HELP FROM A HIGHER SOURCE

Calling on a Higher Power

And now you have the power within
To start a new life and live again.

WHEN I SPOKE WITH DANIEL ON THAT PLANE, HE TOLD me that he had recently watched a popular television show where three men spoke about overcoming sexual addiction. He said that not one of them mentioned calling upon a Higher Power. Daniel felt that the liberation that they found might not be lasting without this step, and I am inclined to agree with him.

We can certainly do a lot to overcome addictions with will-power—or "won't power," as some people have called it. It can indeed be powerful to "Just Say No." But many will tell you this is not enough.

Early in our conversation, I asked Daniel, "What helped the most?" He answered simply, "Prayer."

> *Go to him on bended knee,*
> *And seek his power with humility.*
> *Go to him, both morning and night—*
> *Without him you can't win this fight.*
> *Tell him you need his strength and power*
> *To overcome in weakened hour.*

Daniel prayed to Jesus to be delivered of the demon that was clawing at the back of his neck. And Jesus delivered him.

Prayer in its simplest form is conversation with God—talking to God, telling him of our problems and concerns and asking for his help. That help is ever-present, but we do need to ask. It is the law of heaven that the angels and masters can only enter in when we ask them, because they respect our free will.

Prayer in its simplest form is conversation with God—talking to God, sharing our burdens with him, and asking for his help.

Although you may well feel alone when you are fighting an addiction, you need never really be alone. If you make the call, get down on your knees and sincerely ask God to help you, the hosts of heaven can be right there with you. They only need an invitation to enter the battle and fight alongside you. In fact, if you ask them, they will take on the lion's share of the fight.

When calling on a Higher Power to overcome addiction, there are three heavenly beings that you will want to get to know— Jesus the Christ, Archangel Michael and Saint Germain. They are indispensable partners in anyone's fight against addiction.

The Great Physician

DANIEL FOUND AN EVER-PRESENT HELP WHEN HE CALLED upon the master Jesus, the great physician. I believe that Jesus is very close to us all, but we are often the ones who push him away.

Many people get stuck when they hear the name of Jesus. They think of him as distant, perfect, unapproachable—someone they can't relate to. Beyond this, some Christian denominations have tried to make Jesus their exclusive property—they will tell you that unless you subscribe to their particular version of doctrine, you can't have a relationship with Jesus.

I see Jesus quite differently. He is a master for all religions, both East and West. He studied in the East in preparation for his mission in the Holy Land, and he is known there to this day as Saint Issa.*

He was indeed the Christ. Yet the word *Christ* comes from the Greek *christos,* meaning "anointed." A *Christed* one is simply a person who is anointed with the light of the Lord. That light is the universal light—the light "which lighteth every man that cometh into the world."

Jesus never said he was the only son of God. In fact, John, the closest apostle to Jesus, said that we can all aspire to that calling when he wrote, "Now are we the sons of God ..."

We all have the same light of Christ within us—a divine spark that lives within the heart. The difference between Jesus and

---

*Elizabeth Clare Prophet has chronicled Jesus' journey to the East as a youth in her book *The Lost Years of Jesus.*

most people is that Jesus fully embodied that Christ presence. He had realized that potential, and this is something that we can all strive for—the path that the mystics of all ages have pursued.

Jesus is someone like us, who lived on earth in many lifetimes, as we all have. He knew the challenges of life. He is a friend, a brother who walked the path before us, who now offers to help us find our own way Home. If we call to him, put our trust in him, he can powerfully help us to overcome the dark forces behind addiction. He helped Daniel, and he has helped so many others find their way from the darkness to the light.

As you give these affirmations, Jesus can reinforce your true self and lend you his momentum of victory over every negative condition.

TRANSFIGURING AFFIRMATIONS
of Jesus the Christ

I AM that I AM
I AM the open door which no man can shut
I AM the light which lighteth every man that
    cometh into the world
I AM the way
I AM the truth
I AM the life
I AM the resurrection
I AM the ascension in the light
I AM the fulfillment of all my needs and
    requirements of the hour
I AM abundant supply poured out upon all life
I AM perfect sight and hearing
I AM the manifest perfection of Being
I AM the illimitable light of God made manifest
    everywhere
I AM the light of the Holy of holies
I AM a son of God
I AM the light in the holy mountain of God

Archangel Michael—Your Best Friend

E VERY ANGEL AND MASTER IN HEAVEN KNOWS ARCHANGEL Michael, the archangel of protection, and our souls have also known him for eons. Jewish, Christian and Islamic scriptures all revere Archangel Michael. In fact, Archangel Michael is the best friend anyone could have. In answer to your call, he will protect you and your loved ones each day. He will also stand beside you or a loved one to battle the demons and entities of addiction.

Michael's assignment is to protect those of the light everywhere. He doesn't care what your belief system or religion is—or if you have none at all—but he can help you more effectively if you ask for his assistance. Like all the angels, he respects your free will and obeys the cosmic law that says that angels can enter only where they are invited. Even these simple words will instantly bring blue-lightning angels to your side:

Archangel Michael, help me! Help me! Help me!"

If you find you are about to succumb once more to an addiction, if you are in the depths of despair or urgently in need of help, give this SOS. Call to Archangel Michael's legions whenever and wherever their help is needed. Don't be shy. No problem is too small or too great.

You can also call to Archangel Michael and his blue-lightning angels to rescue other souls who are fighting addictions of any kind. His angels will pull them from the depths of the astral plane and cut them free from the entities of addiction. These mighty angels can help them have a sense of hope as well as the will and desire to overcome. (Of course, the angels will not overrule the free will of souls who refuse their help and choose to keep their addictions.) A simple prayer will invite Lord Michael and his legions of blue-lightning angels into your life.

PRAYER TO ARCHANGEL MICHAEL

Archangel Michael, in the name of my Higher Self, I ask for protection for myself, my family and my loved ones this day. I pray for _____(name of the person)_____. Cut him/her free from the entities of _____(name of the addiction)_____ that tie him/her to that habit.

(Add your personal prayers and name any specific problems that need his intercession.)

I leave all in your hands and keeping. Thank you for hearing my prayer. And I ask that this be done according to God's holy will. Amen.

There is no problem of addiction that does not involve entities and demons. That's why addictions are so hard to break. If you are dealing with a teenage son or daughter who has a cocaine or heroin addiction, then you know that you are dealing not alone with the desires and psychology of your loved one.

There are also dozens or hundreds of entities and forces of darkness working to keep that loved one tied to that addiction. You're not just wrestling against the substance and the habit; you're wrestling against these unseen forces. So if you decide to take this on, you may find that you have to take these calls to another level. These forces of darkness are very determined. So you will find that you have to get more determined than they are.

When dealing with possessing entities, you need to call upon the Lord to embolden you. This is not time for meekness. This is the time to command the light to act and implore the archangels and their legions to bind these forces. Say your prayers out loud

Call to Archangel Michael and his blue-lightning angels to rescue you and any other souls who are fighting addictions of any kind.

in full voice and with determination. And then repeat them, reinforcing the call to light—as the monks and holy ones of East and West recite their prayers and chants by the hour.

The following call to Archangel Michael is easy to memorize and has a powerful rhythm. Give it in multiples of three in full voice for yourself or a loved one. Visualize what you are saying coming pass as a tangible reality—the presence of Archangel Michael on every side, cutting you or your loved one free from addiction.

In answer to this call, Michael and his legions of blue-lightning angels come with their swords of blue flame to cut us free from all entities, cutting through the entire coil of addiction, those tight strands of dark energy that surround us when we are bound by enslaving habits. Then we will feel a weight lifting and a freedom that we may have longed for.

ARCHANGEL MICHAEL'S MANTRA FOR PROTECTION

> Lord Michael before,
> Lord Michael behind,
> Lord Michael to the right,
> Lord Michael to the left,
> Lord Michael above,
> Lord Michael below,
> Lord Michael, Lord Michael wherever I go!
> *I AM his love protecting here! (3x)

Even when we make this call, we will still have to do our part—make right choices, overcome our own habits and momentums. But when we have been cut free from the forces of darkness, we can make those choices free from the aggressive mental suggestion they project at us.

Gradually—and sometimes quite suddenly—as we call upon Archangel Michael each day, we will find that we are influenced less by ties to the underworld as those connections are removed, strand by strand, by this mighty archangel.

The Power to Cast Out Evil Spirits

THE FOLLOWING PRAYER TO ARCHANGEL MICHAEL IS A formula for exorcism that can be used by anyone. It was composed by Pope Leo XIII, who directed that it be included in all Catholic masses. The following version has been adapted for the challenges of this time. Try giving it nine times daily or more, and see how you or a loved one can be delivered from addictions.

POPE LEO'S PRAYER TO ARCHANGEL MICHAEL

Saint Michael the Archangel, defend us in Armageddon. Be our protection against the wickedness and snares of the devil. May God rebuke him, we humbly pray. And do thou, O Prince of the heavenly host, by the power of God, bind the forces of Death and Hell, the seed of Satan, the false hierarchy of Antichrist, and all evil spirits who wander through the world for the ruin of souls, and remand them to the Court of the Sacred Fire for their Final Judgment [including _____*].

Cast out the dark ones and their darkness, the evildoers and their evil words and works, cause, effect, record and memory, into the lake of sacred fire "prepared for the devil and his angels."

In the name of the Father, the Son, the Holy Spirit and the Mother, Amen.

---

*On the first repetition, insert your personal prayer here. Include the names of the entities associated with the addiction—for example, "Spiritus, Spirita, and all alcohol entities." Then repeat the prayer without this insert.

The Angels' Role to Challenge Evil

I T IS IMPORTANT THAT WE ARE VERY CLEAR ABOUT OUR ROLE
when dealing with the forces of darkness behind addiction. It
is not for nothing that entities have been called *demons* in the
religious traditions of East and West. Many of them are indeed
tied to the fallen angels.

The evil spirits associated with addictions can range from
run-of-the-mill discarnates to mischievous demons all the way to
the false hierarchy of archdeceivers or the highest orders of fallen
angels under Lucifer, Satan, Beelzebub and many other chieftains
in the ranks of darkness.

It is not our place to confront this evil. It is the role of
the angels under the direction of the mighty archangels to deal
directly with these forces of darkness. Our role is to "make the
call" that summons these angels into action.

It is never wise to personally challenge evil spirits or to cast
them out by your own authority—to rush in where angels fear to
tread. Many of the seed of the Wicked One have greater attainment on the left-handed path than your attainment in the use of
God's light. It requires someone of equal or greater attainment
in the light to deal with these dark forces.

Therefore, we make the call for those who have that attainment in the light to fight on our behalf. This is why we have been
taught to call on the name of Jesus Christ. This is why we invoke
the assistance of Archangel Michael and his sword of blue flame.

Archangel Michael has fashioned a spiritual sword of blue
flame from pure electric blue-white fire substance, and he wields

this sword for our protection against the forces of evil. You and I are no direct match for Satan and his fallen angels. But Archangel Michael is.

Remember, it is the job of the angels to take on the entities and demons. It is our job to make the call.

It is also important to remember that when you go after these entities of addiction in other people you must have on your own aura sealed and protected. You must have your full armor of light.

When you deal with the dragon of the discarnates who hold people in bondage in addiction, you do have a wrestling match on your hands. In answer to your calls and decrees, the light of God and the angels will go into those conditions and bind the forces of darkness. But you must stand in the midst of the battle being

It is never wise to personally challenge evil spirits or to cast them out by your own authority—to rush in where angels fear to tread.

able to resist the attack of the dragon back upon you before it succumbs and dies.

If the beast finds itself being attacked as a result of your invocations and decrees and it can no longer hold on to its victim, it may turn right around and launch an attack upon you, perhaps in that moment, perhaps within twelve or twenty-four hours after you have made the call.

It will not necessarily attack you with the desire to partake of that addiction. It may be much more subtle than this. It can come in the form of doubt of your spiritual path, doubt in the existence of Archangel Michael and his ability to protect you. You may find yourself getting irritable or angry with other people for no reason. You may face temptations in your own points of weakness. All of these things can separate you from the source of your light, put you off guard, and get you to lose your contact with the light of God and the protection of the angels.

To be a true healer of souls, you have to strive daily to eliminate points of vulnerability. If you are seeking to cut someone free from the alcohol entity, a seemingly small indulgence, like the occasional social drink, can become an opening for an entity to enter. Fear or anxiety can also take from you that necessary point of contact with the hosts of light in the moment when you are the only thing that stands between a soul who is caught in addiction and his continued downward course.

When you invoke the forces of light in the battle against addiction, you become the instrument of the Christ to save a soul from these forces that seek to destroy not only the physical body, but the soul itself if they can. But when you take up this work on behalf of others, it is important to have your own spiritual armor strong.

Here is another powerful call to invoke the presence of Archangel Michael and his protection with you throughout the day. Give the preamble of the decree once, then give your personal prayers. Give the body of the decree as many times as you wish, then conclude the decree with the sealing paragraph.

Many devotees of this great archangel give this decree forty times each day, and many can attest to the miracles of grace and protection they see in their lives through it.

LORD MICHAEL

In the name of the beloved mighty victorious Presence of God, I AM in me, my very own beloved Holy Christ Self, Holy Christ Selves of all mankind, beloved Archangel Michael and all the angels of protection, I decree:

1.   Lord Michael, Lord Michael,
   I call unto thee—
   Wield thy sword of blue flame
   And now cut me free!

Refrain: Blaze God-power, protection
   Now into my world,
   Thy banner of Faith
   Above me unfurl!
   Transcendent blue lightning
   Now flash through my soul,
   I AM by God's mercy
   Made radiant and whole!

2.   Lord Michael, Lord Michael,
   I love thee, I do—
   With all thy great Faith
   My being imbue!

3.   Lord Michael, Lord Michael
   And legions of blue—
   Come seal me, now keep me
   Faithful and true!

Coda: I AM with thy blue flame
   Now full-charged and blest,
   I AM now in Michael's
   Blue-flame armor dressed! (3x)

And in full Faith I consciously accept this manifest, manifest, manifest! (3x) right here and now with full Power, eternally sustained, all-powerfully active, ever expanding, and world enfolding until all are wholly ascended in the Light and free!

Beloved I AM! Beloved I AM! Beloved I AM!

Saint Germain

I F THERE WAS EVER A BEING IN HEAVEN WHO CAN ASSIST YOU in overcoming addiction, it is the ascended master Saint Germain. His name means "holy brother," and that is indeed who he is—a brother to all who are fighting to find their freedom in this life.

Every master and angel in heaven has a heart of love. The heart of a master is a sacred heart. Saint Germain offers his heart and the momentum of his attainment to help those who are struggling with addictions. In an address through Elizabeth Clare Prophet, the master spoke of what is necessary to overcome addiction:

> There is a need to change by the *will of the heart,* by a heart that loves enough to change because others are still suffering from a dishonest expression that you period-ically give vent to....
>
> Beloved hearts, I will stand, and I will stand for eternity, to champion your soul's path of victory and the ascension. Many of you who find yourselves in a pre-carious situation through your dalliance with the carnal mind may this day shed it in this heart and in my heart. For my heart is great enough, as the heart of God, to consume it all.
>
> My heart this day is a cosmic incinerator, if you will, and it can consume if you let go. But remember, it is not a one-time event. You may decide to stop smoking now

Saint Germain offers his heart and the momentum of his attainment to help those who are struggling with addictions.

and put it into my heart, and the record will be consumed. Twenty-four hours from now you will meet the world momentum for which you have had a weakness and you will have to say:

No! Thus far and *no* farther! I shove you back, you nicotine entity! Be *bound* by the power of my heart that is one with the heart of Saint Germain! *You* cannot *touch* me, for I AM the Infinite One! I live in the heart of God. There is no time and space here, and *you* may not dwell in Infinity! And since I do not dwell where you are, I will not smoke today or tomorrow or forever. For I am in my House of Light, and the only smoke that is here is the sweet incense of El Morya* with me!...

---

*El Morya is an ascended master, friend of Saint Germain, teacher of Mark and Elizabeth Clare Prophet and founder of their spiritual organization, The Summit Lighthouse. His great devotion is to the will of God.

Beloved ones, if you remove yourselves from time and space and always find the center of the cross, you will dwell forevermore in the house of the Lord, the secret chamber of the heart, the sacred heart of Jesus, whose heart I have made my own, imploring that Christ and therefore intensifying the purple fiery heart in his honor.

In that heart there is no desire for hashish, there is no desire for heroin. But if you stray from that heart and you have had a long habit, you may identify once again with the outer man or woman and the desiring and find yourself in the turbulent waters, sinking beneath the waves, crying out for the hand of Christ, who will always extend to you that hand until you are safe and sound again in the Heart of Infinity.

You see, beloved ones, all desires of the human that you may have in this world can be surrendered. And when they are surrendered, the divine desiring of God comes into your life. For every human desire there is a divine desire that is legitimate, that is fulfilling, that will give to you whatever you thought you might get through human desiring but truly could never have or keep and much, much more. But it takes courage....

Every experience in life can be transmuted and transcended to become a divine experience.

The section in bold is a prayer that you can give for any addiction, for Saint Germain's offer and his teaching applies to all.

Saint Germain's special gift to us is the violet flame, a spiritual light that acts to transform the negatives in our world. Many who have sought to overcome addiction have found the violet flame to be indispensable to their spiritual and physical progress.

The Violet Flame

THE VIOLET FLAME IS THE SEVENTH RAY ASPECT OF THE Holy Spirit. It is the flame of change, transformation, alchemy and freedom.

The transforming energy of the violet flame can penetrate the thought patterns and momentums that revolve around addiction and change them into patterns of light. It can go into the emotions and feelings that surround addiction—whether the desire for the substance or the feelings of hopelessness, guilt and shame that accompany addiction—and transform them into positive feelings. It can dissolve cravings and transform them into a peaceful and calm sense of victory and overcoming. It can also act to dissolve the dark strands of addiction that have wound around the coil of being.

> *The greatest gift you can give yourself is to invoke the violet flame. It will assist when no other method or tool can.*
>
> —JENNY

The entities and forces of darkness are not comfortable in the presence of this spiritual light. Just as incense has been used for thousands of years to clear churches and temples of dark spirits, so the violet flame blows through the body temple removing all unlike itself.

It is very simple to use the violet flame. Saint Germain has released a number of mantras you can use to invoke the violet flame into your world through the science of the spoken Word. The words of each mantra key you into the visualizations that

that go with them. Here is an easy one to memorize:

I AM a being of violet fire!
I AM the purity God desires!

This simple mantra uses the higher power of your Higher Self, your I AM Presence, to affirm that you are composed of light substance, specifically the violet transmuting flame. It enables the violet fire to flow into your world, to burn through and replace all impurity with the purity that you are at inner levels, affirming that the unwholesome desires of addiction are replaced by God's desires for you.

If you use it regularly, the violet flame can consume the entire momentum of the misuse of God's light and energy that makes up an addiction. It can consume the effects of that addiction in the mind and emotions, the desires and the physical body, greatly enhancing the practical steps you take to overcome addiction. The end result is a new sense of freedom and lightness.

The violet flame is an excellent adjunct to healing any form of addiction. Why not try it for a period of time and watch the results? You have nothing to lose and you may have much to gain.

Transmuting the Past

WHEN I WAS SPEAKING WITH DANIEL, HE TOLD ME HOW the habit of pornography seemed to have become an integral part of his family. It had come to him from his grandfather, and he told me of a number of his immediate family members who were suffering from the same addiction. We spoke of the concept in the Bible of the sins of the fathers being visited on the sons.

I knew that Daniel, a member of the Church of the Latter Day Saints, understood the concept of praying for all the members of one's family tree. I therefore spoke to him about using the energy of the Holy Spirit to go back into the past generations of his family to transmute this entire momentum, back to its very inception. I spoke about how the Holy Spirit can change not only the present but also the past, so bringing about a better tomorrow.

We are all the products of our past. The decisions we have made and the actions we have taken in this and all previous lifetimes have created who we are today. It may seem that what is past is past, that these things cannot be changed. But one of the amazing properties of the violet flame is that it can actually go back to change these momentums and their effects today.

Saint Germain, the master alchemist, has a tremendous momentum in the use of the violet flame. When you give any of the violet-flame mantras in this book, you give him an open door to release the violet flame from his heart to help you. Throw all your problems into the violet flame and let fire of his heart shine through your heart to dissolve them.

The Holy Spirit has its own innate intelligence. The violet flame, as an aspect of the Holy Spirit, knows where to go and what to do to bring about change. It can go to the very source of a problem and dissolve it at its cause and core.

To do this, compose your own prayer to direct the violet flame into those specific conditions and circumstances of the past.

In the name of my own I AM Presence and Holy Christ Self, beloved Saint Germain, send the violet flame into the following conditions:

Name whatever conditions of addiction or other problems you want the violet flame to change. Then give mantras to the violet flame and imagine it going into all of those situations, changing everything into light.

I AM THE LIGHT OF THE HEART
by Saint Germain

I AM the Light of the Heart
Shining in the darkness of being
And changing all into the golden treasury
Of the Mind of Christ.

I AM projecting my Love
Out into the world
To erase all errors
And to break down all barriers.

I AM the power of infinite Love,
Amplifying itself
Until it is victorious,
World without end!

The Science of the Spoken Word

FOR THOUSANDS OF YEARS, THE POWER OF SPOKEN PRAYER for spiritual transformation has been well known. People in the East have repeated their chants and mantras. Those in the West have recited the Our Father and the Rosary. In this age the ascended masters have given a deeper understanding of the power of spoken prayer through what they have called the science of the spoken Word.

One aspect of the science of the spoken Word is the use of the name of God, "I AM." When Moses heard the voice of God speaking to him out of the burning bush, he asked, "What is your name? Who shall I say sent me?" God replied, "Tell them 'I AM' has sent you. I AM THAT I AM. This is my name forever."

When added to prayer, the science of the spoken Word can systematically go to work at the cause and core of the spiritual problems behind addiction.

Many people use affirmations as a means of self-help, of achieving what they want in life. They affirm what they want to manifest, and they find that it comes to pass. When we realize that "I AM" is the name of God, we see that there is more to this than simply reprogramming the subconscious.

Whenever we say "I am," we are invoking the light of our own Higher Self, our own I AM Presence, which is the upper figure in the Chart of Your Divine Self (page 34). We are putting that energy into whatever words follow.

If we say, "I am unhappy," this is what we will manifest. If we say, "I am happy," the power of our I AM Presence will bring it to pass. In this way we can use the power of the name of God to bring about change—both physical and spiritual.

Here is another "I AM" mantra to invoke the violet flame:

I AM THE VIOLET FLAME

I AM the violet flame
  In action in me now
I AM the violet flame
  To light alone I bow
I AM the violet flame
  In mighty cosmic power
I AM the light of God
  Shining every hour
I AM the violet flame
  Blazing like a sun
I AM God's sacred power
  Freeing every one

As you give these words, see the violet flame all around you, clearing your aura, transmuting all the burdens in your life. Even more than this, *feel* the violet flame all around you. Feel its joy and freedom. Even if it is just a flicker of a feeling initially, it can grow. And the more you fill the mantra with feeling, the more quickly what you affirm will come to pass.

When added to prayer, the science of the spoken Word can systematically go to work at the cause and core of the spiritual problems behind addiction. When I was speaking with Daniel, I told him something of this science because I believed that it would provide an action that would add to his own spiritual work. I felt that it could bring him to an even higher place in his overcoming and a new level of healing and freedom.

A Forcefield of Protection

A T TIMES WE CAN ALL FEEL NAKED AND UNPROTECTED, vulnerable to the forces that prey upon the delicate energies of the soul. We all need a place that is safe, apart from the energies of the world. We might have a special place where we can go or even a portion of our home where we can retreat to meditate and pray or just to be.

But we can't stay in our private retreat all the time. We need to get out and engage in the world, to balance our karma and fulfill our mission. So we need a forcefield of protection that we can take with us each day. In fact, all of us, every day, would be wise to guard ourselves from unseen forces by establishing a strong forcefield of light around us.

The Tube of Light is a seamless garment, descending from your I AM Presence all around you like a shimmering waterfall of light.

Archangel Michael can establish a forcefield of blue pro-tective light around you in answer to your prayer. You can call forth additional protection and sealing for your aura through a forcefield of white light around you that is known as the Tube of Light.

When you invoke it, your Tube of Light descends from your I AM Presence around you like a shimmering waterfall of light. It seals you from the mass consciousness and the energies of the world, forming a barrier to darkness and the aggressive energies of the world. It helps to keep out the voices of the night, the entities that whisper in your ear trying to entice you to indulge in negative habits.

TUBE OF LIGHT

Beloved I AM Presence bright,
Round me seal your tube of light
From ascended master flame
Called forth now in God's own name.
Let it keep my temple free
From all discord sent to me.

I AM calling forth violet fire
To blaze and transmute all desire,
Keeping on in freedom's name
Till I AM one with the violet flame.

As you give this decree, imagine your Higher Self above you with the Tube of Light all around you, just as you see it illustrated in the Chart of Your Divine Self on page 34.

God once prophesied of the nation Israel, "I will be a wall of fire round about and the glory in the midst of her." The wall of fire is the Tube of Light, the glory in the midst is the violet flame, and this prophecy is not only for the nation of Israel but for all of us. The Tube of Light is reinforced by the action of the blue-flame protection of Archangel Michael.

"The Violet Flame Is the Key!"

Jenny Hunter

IN THE GRIPS OF ADDICTION, OUR VERY THOUGHTS WERE addicted to creating negatives and thus perpetuating our disease and creating pain, misery and suffering for ourselves and those around us. Look at the power of our destructive thoughts. The mind is the greatest asset we have in overcoming addiction, even though at first it will seem as if we are trying to tame a raging bull.

There are millions in recovery, and they are looking for answers. They say that there is no easy way, but believe me, a simple decree to the violet flame will assist you when nothing else can. I have learned that we can actually change or transmute our past spiritually. We must learn from the past, but also send the violet flame through it. We must become the perfect child of God, the son or daughter of God that has always been inside of us. I have found that with the violet flame we can do exactly that.

Peace of mind is the greatest gift. You were not created to live disconnected and in constant fear, sickness and worry. The same flame that burns on the altar of God is the flame that burns within your heart. You have the power within, but until now you did not know how to use it.

In my estimation our only salvation is the violet flame. Thank goodness I was willing to go outside my comfort zone and learn some simple violet-flame decrees. I encourage fellow addicts or alcoholics to explore the violet flame. It was a key for me in overcoming addiction. It can be a key for you also.

The Divine Mother—East and West

ALL THAT EXISTS WITHIN OUR PHYSICAL WORLD, EVEN the earth body itself, is matter. We can think of this as *mater*, the Latin word for "mother." All of this is part of the feminine aspect of God's being. In the Hindu tradition, the feminine aspect of God is known as *Shakti*. In the Jewish tradition of the Kabbalah, it is known as the *Shekinah*.

Our physical bodies are made of matter—Mother energy—and the light in our spiritual centers is ultimately the light of the Divine Mother. When we have an addiction and we lose the energy in our spiritual centers, it is the light of the Divine Mother that we are wasting. Ultimately we must all resolve our issues with the Divine Mother and the flow of the Mother energy within us, and finding this resolution is an important step for all who are trying to overcome addiction.

The Divine Mother is a person as well as a principle, and there are two mothers in heaven who are so helpful to us in our striving on the spiritual path to overcome addiction. One of these is Mary, the mother of Jesus. Mary's powers of intercession are legendary, and she has appeared throughout the world over and over again to intercede for her children. She is also known as a great healer.

This representative of the Divine Mother has walked the earth as we do. She knows the burdens and trials of life, and she can intercede for us in time of trouble. She can especially assist us as we give the prayer to her, the Hail Mary, the principal prayer of the rosary.

During the giving of the Hail Mary, angels who are called "the weavers" can come to attend the soul whose aura has been damaged by addiction. These angels weave delicate strands of light to replace the threads of darkness of addiction and to mend the holes in the garments of the aura and the spiritual centers.

This prayer has been said for more than a thousand years throughout the Christian world, and it can be a great comfort to those of any faith when struggling to overcome addiction. It gently raises the light of the chakras from the base of the spine to the crown.

HAIL MARY

Hail Mary, full of grace,
The Lord is with thee.
Blessed art thou among women
    and blessed is the fruit of thy womb, Jesus.

Holy Mary Mother of God,
Pray for us sons and daughters of God.
Now and at the hour of our victory
    over sin, disease and death.

You will note that in this version of the prayer, we affirm that we are "sons and daughters of God" instead of "sinners." We also affirm "the hour of our victory over sin, disease and death" instead of "the hour of our death." This is a prayer for a new age —a time when we seek to move beyond the sorrows of the *via dolorosa* and to walk a joyful path of reunion with God through the violet flame.

During the giving of the Hail Mary, angels who are called "the weavers" can come to attend the soul whose aura has been damaged by addiction. These angels weave delicate strands of light to replace the threads of darkness of addiction when they are removed and to mend the holes in the garments of the aura and the spiritual centers. These angel weavers are experts—when they fill in the holes you would never know that there was a tear there. They assist with the weaving of the seamless garment, without which we cannot ascend to God.

Here is a call that you can give to the angel weavers to mend your garments.

PRAYER TO THE ANGEL WEAVERS

In the name of my Mighty I AM Presence and beloved Mary, I call to the angels who are the expert weavers to mend and heal the rents in my seamless garment, in my chakras, my aura and forcefield, my entire consciousness, being and world.

I pray for intercession and I ask for these angels to weave threads of light and to remove the threads of darkness placed there by unwise sowings from this or past lives.

I accept it done this hour in full power according to God's Holy Will. Amen.

Kuan Yin, Mother of Mercy

ANOTHER DIVINE MOTHER, A FAVORITE OF MANY IN THE East, is Kuan Yin. Devotion to her runs very deep throughout China and Japan. She is known to many as the court of last resort in heaven. Her name means "one who hears the cries of the world," and when you cannot seem to get a response from anyone else, Kuan Yin may be the one who can deliver you from a very difficult situation.

Kuan Yin is revered as a mother figure and divine mediator. Many think of her as a Buddhist Madonna—just as Mary, the mother of Jesus, is the Madonna in the West. She is also a Bodhisattva, which means she has forsaken the pleasures of nirvana to remain with earth's evolutions until all are free.

Buddhists know Kuan Yin as one who guides souls to salvation across the troubled ocean of existence. She stands on the "Barque of Salvation" guiding souls to the Western Paradise, or Pure Land, a celestial realm of bliss. She is known for her ability to save souls shipwrecked on the shores of life (an accurate description of the state of addiction).

Here is a simple mantra to Kuan Yin, one of many that are available to call for her assistance. This mantra can be said many times, especially in multiples of three:

NA-MO KUAN SHIH YIN P'U-SA*

This mantra means: "Hail! (Homage to the sacred name of) Bodhisattva Kuan Shih Yin."

---

*This mantra is pronounced: NAH-MO GWAN SHE(R) EEN POO-SAH. (R) indicates a light *r*.

*When you cannot seem
to get a response from
anyone else in heaven,
Kuan Yin may be the one
who can deliver you
from a very difficult
situation. Many believe
that simply saying her
name over and over will
bring her instantly to
their side.*

Kuan Yin is known for her miracles, particularly for the miracle of a changed heart. She can also plead for souls before the courts of heaven, imploring mercy and renewed opportunity.

She is known as the Bodhisattva of Compassion and the Goddess of Mercy. We can call to her when it is hard to forgive ourselves or others. Her flame of mercy can help us let go of the hurts of the past and make a new start.

Kuan Yin's devotees believe completely in her saving grace, and she is respected for her powerful ability to heal body, mind and soul. Many believe that simply saying her name over and over will bring her instantly to their side.

Exorcism through the Starry Mother

ANY DISCUSSION OF SPIRITUAL TOOLS TO HELP OVERCOME addiction would not be complete without speaking of Astrea, who is known as the "Starry Mother." Astrea is a feminine aspect of God, a cosmic being, one of whose specialties is dealing with entities and demons. When you are wrestling with an entity that already has its tentacles into you or someone you love, there is no more powerful call than the one to Astrea.

When you are wrestling with an entity that already has its tentacles into you or someone you love, there is no more powerful call than the one to Astrea.

The powerful mantra to Astrea on the next page can be used on behalf of any and all who are caught in the grips of the entities of addiction. I have seen remarkable results of almost miraculous deliverance when groups of people gathered and gave this prayer together. Many people have been cut free permanently from all forms of addiction by Archangel Michael and Astrea, who wield their swords of blue flame to bind the entities and demons behind addiction.

Give your personal prayer following the preamble of this decree, naming the specific condition or addiction (including the name of the entity) you are working on.

DECREE TO BELOVED MIGHTY ASTREA
"The Starry Mother"

In the name of the beloved Mighty Victorious Presence of God, I AM in me, Mighty I AM Presence and Holy Christ Selves of all mankind, by and through the magnetic power of the sacred fire vested in the Threefold Flame burning within my heart, I call to beloved Mighty Astrea, the entire Spirit of the Great White Brotherhood and the World Mother, elemental life—fire, air, water and earth! to lock your cosmic circles and swords of blue flame in, through and around my four lower bodies, my electronic belt, my heart chakra and all of my chakras, my entire consciousness, being and world.

[Give your personal prayers here.]

Cut me loose and set me free (3x) from all that is less than God's perfection and my own divine plan fulfilled.

    1. O beloved Astrea, may God Purity
       Manifest here for all to see,
       God's divine Will shining through
       Circle and sword of brightest blue.

First chorus: Come now answer this my call,
       Lock thy circle round us all.
       Circle and sword of brightest blue,
       Blaze now, raise now, shine right through!

    2. Cutting life free from patterns unwise,
       Burdens fall off while souls arise
       Into thine arms of infinite Love,
       Merciful shining from heaven above.

    3. Circle and sword of Astrea now shine,
       Blazing blue-white my being refine,
       Stripping away all doubt and fear,
       Faith and goodwill patterns appear.

119

Second chorus: Come now answer this my call,
Lock thy circle round us all.
Circle and sword of brightest blue,
Raise our youth now, blaze right through!

Third chorus: Come now answer this my call,
Lock thy circle round us all.
Circle and sword of brightest blue,
Raise mankind now, shine right through!

And in full Faith I consciously accept this manifest, manifest, manifest! (3x) right here and now with full Power, eternally sustained, all-powerfully active, ever expanding and world enfolding until all are wholly ascended in the Light and free!

Beloved I AM! Beloved I AM! Beloved I AM!

After giving the preamble, give verses 1, 2 and 3, each followed by the first chorus. Then give verses 1, 2 and 3, each followed by the second chorus. Next give verses 1, 2 and 3, each followed by the third chorus. Give this pattern as many times as you wish, then conclude with the ending to seal the action of the decree.

Kuthumi, the Master Psychologist

THERE IS A HEAVENLY MASTER WHO IS AN EXPERT IN HELP-ing people overcome addictions. His name is Kuthumi. Many people know him from his embodiment as Francis of Assisi, one of the most beloved saints of the West. You can call to him for peace, enlightenment and understanding.

Kuthumi can assist you with any kind of personal problem—mental, emotional, physical, spiritual or psychological. His special gift is to assist you with your physical health and healing and also with your personal psychology or karmic circumstances. You can ask him to overshadow any therapist or counselor or health professional you are working with.

This beloved master understands the human condition and the nature of the lesser self. He also sees your Higher Self and all that you are already from a spiritual perspective. He desires to see you become who you really are. His gentle and peaceful aura provides comfort and strength. A simple prayer will give him permission to enter your heart and your world. If you give his "I AM Light" decree, he can help you even more.

Many people have used this affirmation to help them over-come addiction. As you give it, visualize, with the power of your imagination, the beautiful concepts it contains as vividly as you can. Feel them becoming real within you as you speak the words. See any darkness being swallowed up by the mighty river of light.

Repeat this prayer as a mantra until you feel its purpose has been accomplished within you at that moment. Then return to it daily, or more often as you feel the need, for the pattern to be

Kuthumi's special gift is to assist you with your physical health and healing, and with your personal psychology or karmic circumstances.

strengthened. You will thereby build coils of light in your aura to replace the coils of darkness of negative habits and addictions.

I AM LIGHT
by Kuthumi

I AM light, glowing light,
Radiating light, intensified light.
God consumes my darkness,
Transmuting it into light.

This day I AM a focus of the Central Sun.
Flowing through me is a crystal river,
A living fountain of light
That can never be qualified
By human thought and feeling.
I AM an outpost of the Divine.
Such darkness as has used me is swallowed up
By the mighty river of light which I AM.

I AM, I AM, I AM light;
I live, I live, I live in light.
I AM light's fullest dimension;
I AM light's purest intention.
I AM light, light, light
Flooding the world everywhere I move,
Blessing, strengthening and conveying
The purpose of the kingdom of heaven.

If you ever have the opportunity to visit the town of Assisi, you will feel the powerful and peaceful presence of Saint Francis there. But you don't need to go to Italy to feel his presence. As you give this prayer, you are not only calling for the light of your own I AM Presence. You also form a tie to the heart of Kuthumi, whose words these are, and his momentum of light can strengthen you in overcoming all addictions and problems in your life.

The same is true of all the prayers and mantras that have been given by the great masters: giving their words brings their presence to us, connecting us with their momentum of light.

Transfiguring Change

ALMOST EVERYONE I MEET WHO STRUGGLES WITH ADDIC-
tion wants to change. Most long for a clean break, a
new start. The following mantra invokes the light of the
transfiguration, an experience in the life of Jesus. The Bible
records that on the Mount of Transfiguration, Jesus' face shone
like lightning and his garments became glistering white. The light
of his I AM Presence descended and his whole form was changed,
even the clothes he was wearing.

We can also experience transfiguring change. We can call for
the light of our own I AM Presence to change our darkness to
light. We may not experience an instantaneous change, as Jesus
did. But day by day, we can put off our old garments of negative
habits, self-belittlement and condemnation and put on the robe,
the inner garment, of our Christ consciousness.

TRANSFIGURATION

I AM changing all my garments,
Old ones for the bright new day;
With the sun of understanding
I AM shining all the way.

I AM light within, without;
I AM light is all about.
Fill me, free me, glorify me!
Seal me, heal me, purify me!
Until transfigured they describe me:
I AM shining like the Son,
I AM shining like the Sun! (3x)

The Flame of Illumination

IN THE SECTION ON MARIJUANA, WE SPOKE OF THE LONG-TERM effects of the drug on those who used it in their teenage years, including a much higher incidence of schizophrenia ten or more years later. Another long-term effect is a lingering dullness and depression. Many who give up this drug find that it takes months or years to regain the clarity of thought they knew before they used it.

These effects are signs of the physical effects of addiction on the brain, which may be the result of chemical residues or disruptions in chemistry or structure. These physical effects also reflect what has happened to the finer bodies and the chakras, which need to be cleared of residues and healed of damage.

The following decree can be used for the healing of the crown, the third eye and the physical brain, particularly from the effects of drugs of all kinds. It is easy to memorize. Give it as a mantra throughout the day as you visualize the golden light of the sun around you. The flame of illumination is a very joyful flame—the perfect antidote to the depression and anxiety that often arise in withdrawal from any addiction.

> O Flame of Light bright and gold,
> O Flame most wondrous to behold,
> I AM in every brain cell shining,
> I AM in Light's wisdom all divining.
> Ceaseless, flowing fount of illumination's flaming,
> I AM, I AM, I AM Illumination.

The Real Work of Overcoming Addiction

IT IS GENERALLY BELIEVED THAT THE SUCCESS RATE IN OVER-coming serious addictions is about one in ten. Based on Jenny's experience, she estimates it is closer to one in fifteen. I believe that this reflects the limitations of the tools and strategies that have been used in the battle against addiction.

It is well known that willpower alone is not enough to overcome addiction. We also see the shortcomings of counselling and intensive therapy in the lives of Hollywood stars and their repeated visits to rehab. A common limitation of these approaches is that they draw primarily from human resources—the strength that the individual can find within or the skill and dedication of those who seek to help.

These factors are important, and often vital. But something more is often needed to win the battle—and that is the spiritual dimension, and especially dealing with the unseen forces behind addiction. Twelve-Step programs open the door to spiritual help by encouraging participants to turn themselves over to God and pray for his strength. This is a good first step, but there is a science of spirituality that can take this to another level.

The science of the spoken Word and the sword of the Spirit are often the missing dimension in overcoming addiction. These

The science of the spoken Word and the sword of the Spirit are often the missing dimension in overcoming addiction. A program to overcome addiction will be most effective if it addresses all levels of the problem— spiritual, mental, emotional and physical.

are not a substitute for practical strategies. In fact, a program to overcome addiction will be most effective if it addresses all levels of the problem—mental, emotional and physical as well as the spiritual.

We will look at some of the most effective mental, emotional and physical tools that can help in overcoming addiction in the next section. Some of these strategies are quite simple to apply, yet they can have surprisingly powerful effects. However, it is important to remember that all of these will be more effective when combined them with work on the spiritual dimension.

PART 7

AN INTEGRATED APPROACH

Healing the Four Lower Bodies

ADDICTION IS A CONDITION THAT AFFECTS ALL OF THE four lower bodies of man, so it makes sense that a holistic approach to addiction can increase your chances for success and reduce the otherwise high rate of relapse.

In the previous section we looked at spiritual tools. These work most directly on levels beyond the physical—especially with the etheric body, which is the inner blueprint for what will manifest in the other three bodies. However, we can also work directly with these other bodies to accelerate the healing process, and because all the bodies are connected, working with all of them will have a synergistic effect.

Science is now beginning to understand the myriad connections between mental, emotional and physical health, and holistic therapies to facilitate the healing of the whole person are becoming much more widely used, even in hospitals and conventional medical settings. Among other benefits, these therapies work to stimulate the body's natural ability to heal.

We will begin this survey with some strategies for healing the physical body, which is intended to be the vehicle for your spirit. It works best when you support it with a healthy diet and exercise.

A Diet for Healing

MANY PEOPLE WHO TREAT ADDICTION ARE NOW recognizing that nutrition has an important role to play in supporting mind, body and spirit in recovery. Alcoholics and those addicted to drugs often eat poorly, and the food that they eat is often fast food with empty calories devoid of true nutrition. As a result, addicts frequently experience a myriad of health problems: central nervous system issues, such as sleeplessness, anxiety and agitation; gastrointestinal complaints such as poor appetite and digestion problems; and many other illnesses. All of these, along with the vitamin and mineral deficiencies from a poor diet, can worsen anxiety and depression, in turn leading to a greater craving for alcohol and other drugs.

One key factor in alcohol and drug abuse compromised by a poor diet is that these prevent the body from correctly processing the vital amino acids tyrosine and tryptophan, which are needed for the production of the neurotransmitters dopamine, serotonin and norepinephrine.

Tyrosine is found in protein-rich foods and is a precursor to dopamine and norepinephrine, which help with mental functioning and alertness. Tryptophan is needed for the production of serotonin, which helps to calm the nervous system and promote sleep. These three neurotransmitters are vital for stability of the emotions, clarity of the mind and a general sense of well-being— all of which are desperately needed by the addict in recovery.

It is well known that addicts in recovery suffer from depression when they come down from the highs of substance abuse.

This is due to lower levels of serotonin and dopamine, which adversely affects mood and aggravates poor behavior. Sometimes recovering addicts turn to sugar and caffeine to compensate, since these have the effect of stimulating neurotransmitters. This fills the gap temporarily, but also causes the same problem of a down after the initial high. These mood swings are counterproductive to the goal of bringing normal functioning to the mind and emotions, and many experts feel that sugar and caffeine can be an open door to relapse.

Specific deficiencies depend partly on the type of addiction. According to David Wiss, founder of Los Angeles–based Nutrition in Recovery, opiate addicts often show deficiencies in calcium, vitamins D and B6, and iron, while cocaine addicts typically have deficiencies in omega-3 fatty acids (another vital nutrient for brain function).

Alcoholics often have more extensive deficiencies, since alcohol causes the body to lose large quantities of nutrients. Ravi Chandiramani, an addiction-treatment expert in Scottsdale, Arizona, explains, "We commonly see B vitamin deficiencies in alcoholics manifested as factor-deficiency anemia. Vitamin K deficiencies manifest as clotting problems and slow-to-heal wounds. Vitamin C deficiencies and mineral deficiencies may also result in slow wound healing and immune system challenges."

It takes time to rebuild depleted body tissues and organ systems that have been damaged by addiction and the lifestyle that often accompanies it. Nutritionists recommend a diet high in protein, complex carbohydrates and healthy fats as well as other essential nutrients. Many nutritionists also recommend reducing or eliminating the intake of caffeine and refined sugars due to the destabilizing effects these can have on brain chemistry.

Vitamins and supplements are often helpful to deal with nutritional deficiencies caused by addiction and poor diet, especially B vitamins and folic acid. Daily vitamin D supplements can be beneficial, since this nutrient is key to many systems in the body. Omega-3 oils play an important part in normalizing the function of nerve cells in the brain and help to stabilize mood. High doses of vitamin C as well as digestive enzymes and other specific supplements recommended by a qualified nutritionist can greatly increase the proper functioning of the body and the alleviation of symptoms.

In the long term, the higher nutrient value of whole foods and organically-grown produce is especially important in recovery. Learning how to prepare meals from quality ingredients has clear health benefits and often costs less than relying on processed foods and fast foods. The daily ritual of preparing food also provides a level of groundedness and stability to life.

Victoria Abel, founder of the Center for Addiction Nutrition, says, "Addiction nutrition along with psychotherapy can have a dramatic and lasting impact when working with clients with addictive disorders. It helps to heal the body as well as the mind and the spirit."

Eating is something that we all do every day. Eating well is something that you can choose to do for yourself, and if you make this choice you will soon see the positive impact on the way you feel and behave as well as in the improved functioning of your body. Preparing your own food in itself can be a healing experience if you do it with love and thoughtfulness.

When you feel and look better through daily right choices in food, it reinforces other right choices in your life. A healthy meal plan and supportive nutrition combined with exercise and other mind-body therapies can be an important foundation for getting on the road to recovery and staying free of drugs, alcohol and other addictions.

Exercise

MANY FORMER ADDICTS ARE FINDING THAT EXERCISE is an important part of their recovery, and many addiction treatment centers now make fitness a key part of their programs. Jennifer Dewey, fitness director for the Betty Ford Center in Rancho Mirage, California, explains that exercise is "one of the critical components of sustaining sobriety."

Exercise can be a useful distraction from obsessing about an addiction, but it is much more than this. Exercise can actually help addicts to overcome physical and emotional withdrawal. In fact, one study found that exercise cut cravings and drug use by more than 50 percent—even with no other treatment.

This seems to be partly the result of the beneficial effects of exercise on brain chemistry. Our brains experience a chemical reward from addictions (behavioral or chemical), and exercise can provide an alternative, healthier reward by increasing the levels of dopamine in the brain in a natural and balanced way, which increases feelings of pleasure and decreases levels of anxiety and stress. In other words, exercise provides a natural high to replace the high from the addiction.

Exercise is well known as a natural anti-depressant. Studies show that exercise during addiction recovery helps addicts to deal with obsessive thoughts and overcome depression. In addition, exercise boosts the immune system, helps remove toxins from the body, improves circulation and burns up the additional weight that many addicts put on during their addictive phase. Exercise improves general health and cardiovascular health. It helps to regulate sleep, which is often an issue for addicts. Former addicts report that exercise keeps their moods stable and helps them to maintain a positive attitude, which makes it easier to stay in recovery.

Another important aspect of exercise is that it often involves increased social interaction and teamwork. By joining a group of people who exercise together, recovering addicts can make new friends and connect with people who live a healthier lifestyle and who can encourage them in setting and accomplishing new goals.

Recovering addicts also report that they enjoy the structure that regular exercise provides. An exercise program by its nature helps you to maintain a schedule, to better organize your life and to keep busy as you create and accomplish your goals. It helps develop accountability, which is something that is often lacking in the lives of addicts. An exercise program gives people something to do in some of those otherwise idle hours when they might be tempted to relapse.

Any kind of exercise can be a benefit: running, team sports, weights, yoga, kickboxing, Pilates, working out at a fitness club, walking in nature or hiking. It doesn't have to be complicated. Studies show that clients who incorporate exercise into their rehab programs report a much reduced intake of drugs. In addition, they look and feel better, have more energy and report that their quality of life is much improved.

Some commentators have pointed out that some former addicts who take up exercise seem to become obsessive about exercise and question whether they have simply replaced one addiction with another. Even if this were true, replacing a harmful addiction such as drugs or alcohol with a healthy one such as exercise would be a step in the right direction. (An exception might be in the case of an eating disorder, where excessive exercise might be part of the addiction itself.)

Even with all its benefits, most experts also say that exercise is not a cure-all. If you become obsessed with exercise but you don't pay attention to learning about yourself, you won't get the same level of healing you might if you also pursue resolution of the emotional pain and other issues underlying addiction. Nevertheless, exercise has been shown to improve the chances that an addict will succeed in quitting, and a drug-free mind and a healthier body provide a much better foundation for the deeper work.

Dan Cronin, an addiction interventionist in Pasadena who uses exercise as a key element of his programs, says, "I see people who not only feel better about themselves, but they feel better about everything."

One innovative program is run by an organization called Phoenix Multisport (phoenixmultisport.org), a support community for those who are recovering from substance abuse. They focus on sports and fitness pursuits such as climbing, hiking, skiing, running, strength training, yoga and road or mountain biking, along with social events and other activities.

If you don't live near one of the facilities this organization operates, there are health and fitness clubs in every city in America. Parks and recreation departments in city governments often have directories of clubs devoted to a multitude of different sports.

Yoga

YOGA EMPOWERS RECOVERING ADDICTS TO FIND A PLACE within themselves that is peaceful and calm. It is a tool that they can use at any time to stay grounded and to help deal with anxiety, stress or depression.

You don't have to become an expert or have a lot of flexibility to experience the many benefits of yoga. Even simple poses can be very helpful. People report feelings of peace, comfort and release as they learn to sit quietly, focus on their breathing, move gently, and calm the body and the mind.

Most private rehabilitation facilities offer some kind of yoga or mind-body awareness program. Jennifer Dewey of the Betty Ford Center explains some of the benefits of these programs: "Addiction takes a person out of their body and prevents them from connecting to who they are physically and feeling what their body is telling them. Yoga is a great way to slowly reintroduce someone to physical sensation. It's also very relaxing."

Yoga can help you tune into the cues that your body is giving you and help you to be more mindful in your responses. One mechanism may be through regulating the stress hormones cortisol and adrenaline, which are often high in people dealing with substance abuse, anxiety disorders, depression and post-traumatic stress disorders.

If you are less stressed you can make better decisions. You will also be less driven to seek substances or other addictions as a means to escape from the pressures of daily life.

Meditation

MEDITATION HAS THE ABILITY TO CALM THE MIND, relax the body, and soothe the soul and spirit— benefits that can help anyone, but especially those who are seeking to overcome an addiction.

Anyone can learn to meditate. People have been practicing meditation for thousands of years in many traditions, East and West, yet you don't have to belong to any particular religion, culture or spiritual path to meditate. The basic techniques are so simple that anyone can learn them. You can select a meditation technique that fits your lifestyle and belief system.

Meditation works best if you can build it into your daily routine. The practice begins with quieting the mind and concentrating on a specific thought or idea. Start with a five-minute meditation session once a day and work up from there. A twenty-minute session twice a day is ideal, but it is not about competition with others or feeling guilty that you didn't meditate long enough. It is about being kind to yourself, appreciating what you can do, and knowing that this can make a difference.

The benefits of meditation are well-documented. Meditation has been proven to help with pain relief, with the inability to sleep, and in dealing with the stresses of daily life. Meditation helps with focus, memory and the ability to maintain a sense of calm.

Studies show that recovering addicts who are taught how to meditate have lower levels of relapse and more positive outcomes. Meditation is even more effective when combined with physical exercise. Addicts report that meditation combined with yoga or the Chinese practice of *chi gung* (which itself incorporates meditative techniques) leads to fewer cravings and less symptoms related to addiction.

There are a number of reasons that meditation is so effective. Neuroscientists are now finding that meditation can cause positive changes even in the physical structure of the brain, rewiring critical nerve pathways. Studies have found that people who meditated for thirty minutes a day for eight weeks showed an increase in gray matter in parts of the brain associated with learning, memory, self-awareness, and introspection as well as a decrease in gray matter in areas of the brain connected to anxiety and stress.

All of this translates into being less reactive to challenging and stressful situations, responding in a more reflective way and making better decisions. These are vital skills for those who are seeking to overcome addiction, because stress and anxiety are often the triggers for relapse. If you slow down your breathing, calm your nerves, feel less stressed or anxious, and reduce those gnawing negative thoughts and feelings, you will be less likely to reach for the substance that you turned to in the past.

And beyond the physical, mental and emotional benefits, there are also the spiritual benefits. Many people who pursue meditation based on a spiritual tradition find that this helps them feel connected to a higher power, and the strength they gain thereby has helped them to stay with their recovery program.

So take some time to meditate each day. Stay focused. Keep breathing. Find that peaceful place inside of you. Make mindfulness and meditation a part of your life.

There are a number of free smartphone apps that give a good introduction to simple techniques along with guided meditations, and these are a good way to start a daily practice. The good news is that even a few minutes a day can make a difference.

A simple meditation

FIND A QUIET PLACE WHERE YOU CAN SIT COMFORTABLY WITHOUT being disturbed. Turn off your cell phone and anything else that might be a distraction.

Close your eyes.

Take a few deep breaths, and then settle into a natural rhythm of breathing.

Observe how the breath moves in and out of your body.

Choose a focus for your meditation—an image or a mantra.

An image or a thoughtform can be anything you choose. It could be as simple as the image of the sun or a rose, your favorite saint or master, or something as complex as the tangkas that Tibetan Buddhists use for their meditations. As you hold this thought in your mind, make it as real as you can. If you are visualizing the sun, see the brightness of the light, feel the warmth of its rays on your skin.

A mantra for meditation can be a very simple phrase or prayer, such as the OM or I AM THAT I AM, or a quality of God, such as PEACE. Hear this sound repeating gently in your mind, as if you are listening to someone else saying it. As you hear it, also *feel* the quality associated with it.

As you hold this image or sound, observe yourself and your body as well as your responses and reactions.

Does your body feel uncomfortable? Simply observe this.

Does your mind wander? Does your attention go to something else? Observe this also.

Don't worry or feel guilty if other thoughts come up—just gently bring your attention back to the focus of your meditation.

At the end of your period of meditation (five minutes, ten minutes, or however long you wish), open your eyes and return to your awareness of the space around you.

Tips for meditation

PEOPLE OFTEN THINK THAT A MEDITATION IS ONLY SUCCESSFUL if you can stay entirely focused on one thing and not have the mind wander at all. However, the wandering of the mind is also part of the process.

Thoughts may arise during your meditation and the mind may wander —simply be aware of this, as you are aware of whatever happens during your meditation. If you are meditating and you feel a feeling or think a thought or have a sensation in your body, simply observe it, acknowledge it, name it, and without judgment, let it pass. Don't hold onto it, but gently return to awareness of your breath and the focus of your meditation.

Meditation works best if you can build it into your daily routine. Start with a five-minute meditation session once a day and work up from there. A twenty-minute session twice a day is ideal. The good news is that only a few minutes a day can make a difference.

Another common misperception about meditation is that it should involve some sort of transcendent or mystical experience. Some people experience these things, but most do not—and in any case, this is not what is important.

This simple form of meditation is not about trying to achieve mystical states. It is just about being still for a while and being mindful of your body, your thoughts and your feelings.

Mindfulness

MANY ADDICTION TREATMENT CENTERS ARE NOW using mindfulness techniques as a key element in their programs. A basic premise of this approach is that instead of trying to avoid or suppress the urge towards an addiction, you are encouraged to pay attention to the physical sensation, observe how the cravings manifest, accept them, and then simply let them go. You acknowledge the craving, but do not act on the urge. Mindfulness techniques are a means to establish new patterns in the mental and emotional bodies to replace the old patterns of addiction.

One excellent book that explores this approach to addiction is *Mindful Recovery: A Spiritual Path to Healing from Addiction,* by Thomas and Beverley Bien. Among the specific techniques they talk about is journaling.

They present this tool as a vehicle for transformation as well as a helpful means of being able to keep track of your progress and observe the ups and downs. Write in your journal when you are doing well, and affirm the progress you are making.

Also write when you are not doing well, because there is a lot to be learned from setbacks. The Biens say, "If you journal about a relapse, it is important to deal with the thoughts, feelings, and events that led to it, and identify alternatives. How else could you view the situation that triggered the relapse, and similar ones? What could you have done differently, said differently, thought differently?" Examining the patterns means that you can learn from them. This makes it possible to change.

The Biens say, "Every once in a while it is helpful to look through your journal entries to gain a perspective on the sweep and movement of your life over time." As you do, you may start to see some themes emerge. They stress journaling without self-judgment and yet exploring your thoughts and feelings, particularly around a temptation to relapse or an actual relapse. "Your journal is the friend that is always there."

Awareness of the breath is a common theme in mindfulness practices and in meditation. Your breath is something that is always there and which you can tune into at any time. If you simply observe your breath, it brings you right back to where you are now rather than revolving the past or worrying about what might happen in the future. As Bien says, "We need ways to be present with life as it is, rather than as we prefer it to be."

If you find yourself in a stressful situation, just consciously breathing more slowly and deeply will in itself shift your mental state, allowing you to deal with the stress from a position of greater peace and centeredness.

Observing your breath can also tell you about your state of mind even before you are aware of it consciously. Tension or stress causes a tightening of the chest and shallower breathing—a natural physiological reaction.

The wonderful thing about working with the mind-body connection is that it works both ways. If you find yourself in a stressful situation, just shifting your awareness to your breath and consciously breathing more slowly and deeply will in itself shift your mental state, allowing you to deal with the stress from a position of greater peace and centeredness.

Thomas and Beverley Bien's *Mindful Recovery* also contains excellent and simple keys on how to meditate and how to be mindful when walking through recovery.

Other Holistic Therapies

THERE ARE MANY HOLISTIC METHODS TO ASSIST IN THE healing of addiction. Many of them work not only with the physical body but also with the body's subtle energy system. All can assist in dealing with the many stresses associated with addiction and also heal underlying imbalances that may have been a factor in taking up an addiction in the first place.

Acupuncture, herbal medicine, aromatherapy, homeopathy, Bach flower remedies, massage and chiropractic treatment have all been found to be adjuncts to support body, mind and spirit through the recovery process. Here are examples of how some of these techniques can help with healing from addiction.

Acupuncture

Acupuncture is a form of Traditional Chinese Medicine which can be used to correct the flow of energy through the body's energy meridians—the pathways through which our vital energy (*qi* or *ch'i*) travels to our organs and through our entire body.

One of the effects of addictions of all kinds is that they disturb the flow of *ch'i* through the body, causing an intense flow and then leaving the body drained and with the *ch'i* stagnant afterwards. By restoring the correct flow of energy, acupuncture can help to restore balance and heal the damage of addiction.

Herbal medicine

Herbal medicines can be used to naturally heal the body, clear the mind and soothe the soul. Herbs often work synergistically in the body and in the right combination can be an effective adjunct to healing the mental and emotional effects of addiction. An experienced naturopath or herbalist can help to determine the appropriate use for each individual.

Aromatherapy

Aromatherapy using essential oils is a wonderful way to support healing on all levels. Essential oils are distilled from the roots, leaves, flowers or seeds of plants. They have been used through the ages to promote health and well-being.

Those who are dealing with addiction suffer from many forms of stress, and they are often prone to infections and all kinds of physical, mental and emotional symptoms. Aromatherapy can support the body in a number of ways, including relaxation when needed, stimulation of circulation for physical healing, and enhancement of immune function. Oils can alleviate stress, fight infections and help relieve pain. The right choice or combination of essential oils can help to strengthen the body so it can heal itself at all levels. Frankincense, spikenard and neroli oil may be especially helpful for those in recovery.

Frankincense improves the immune system, promotes spiritual awareness, assists with meditation, and can support an attitude adjustment that is very helpful when facing a challenging illness or disease such as alcoholism or addiction.

Spikenard is a medicinal herb used traditionally to nourish and regenerate the skin. Spikenard is also known for its ability to assist the soul through difficult initiations, including the dark night of the soul and the dark night of the Spirit. It has a distinctive and powerful fragrance.

Neroli is very useful essential oil to elevate mood and dispel the mental and emotional problems that plague many addicts and alcoholics. Neroli oil is used to lift depression and anxiety, to calm frayed nerves, relax the muscles and to deal with stress. It also has powerful psychological effects. This oil can help us to be present in the moment and to stay calm and focused. It can strengthen and stabilize the emotions and also bring relief to seemingly hopeless situations—appropriate for someone going through recovery from addiction.

Many more essential oils are available, and you may wish to study and experiment to discover the most effective oils for you.

Homeopathy

Homeopathic remedies can be used to restore balance to the body's subtle energy fields. The art and science of homeopathy, when administered by a qualified homeopath, can have deep healing effects at many levels.

Bach flower remedies

Bach flower remedies can help fine tune our emotional state and specifically assist in dealing with a negative emotional outlook. Addicts often experience a mental or emotional rut and have great difficulty getting unstuck. These subtle remedies can help the individual to gently and naturally get past these blocks without harmful side effects. Simply read the descriptions of the individual remedies and the emotional or mental imbalances they address, and choose the ones that fit your needs.

Massage

Massage and other forms of physical therapy can be comforting and soothing to those suffering from addiction. They help to boost the body's intrinsic healing mechanisms and have a calming and soothing effect, physically and emotionally.

There are many other complementary therapies that have been used to help with addiction. Ask your Higher Self to direct you to the most effective forms of therapy for you.

Your Environment

WHEN YOU ARE TRYING TO CHANGE YOUR LIFE, IT IS important to feed your mind a diet of wholesome thoughts. Surround yourself with images that reinforce what you want to be, rather than looking back to where you have come from.

If you are trying to give up drugs, avoid movies and television shows where people are using drugs. And maybe cut down on television as a whole—most people would agree that a steady diet of television is not a healthy way to spend one's time.

Some people find it is very helpful to get rid of as much as possible from their environment that is connected to the life they want to leave behind. For example, getting rid of the clothes you used to wear when you were using drugs removes something that could trigger again the thoughts and feelings of that time. It is also a psychological and symbolic break from the past, a reminder of the inner commitment and a physical sign that change is possible. On a spiritual level, it is removing from your environment those things that may still carry the energy and vibration of activities of the past.

One thing Daniel did to change his environment was his determination not to use a computer again. Another man trying to make a break from porn addiction found that he couldn't have a computer in his bedroom, but if he moved the computer to the living room of the house, where other people might see what he was watching, he wouldn't be tempted.

Create a world around you that reflects the new life you want to live, and this will help to also remake the inner landscape. Spend time each day in environments that support the healing of your physical, mental and emotional bodies.

Spending time in nature can have an especially powerful impact on mental and emotional states. Researchers have found that even watching videos of nature can have noticeable effects. Some prison systems are now using videos of nature to help prisoners deal with the mental and emotional health challenges of solitary confinement. Even better, of course, is to get outside and experience nature directly.

Scientists are now quantifying something we have always known intuitively—that being in nature is healing for body and soul.

Researchers at the Great Outdoor Lab at UC Berkeley are studying the effect of nature on psychological and physical health, and they are finding amazing results. For example, they documented a lasting thirty-five percent reduction in PTSD symptoms in veterans after participating in a single three-day rafting trip.

Scientists are now quantifying something we have always known intuitively—that being in nature is healing for body and soul.

Friends

I REMEMBER A FRIEND WATCHING HER DAUGHTER MAKE SOME poor choices. The mother turned to me and said, "I wish she would choose her friends more carefully." She could see that under the influence of her friends, her daughter was moving into a life that revolved around alcohol.

Although the daughter drank very little, she was dating a man who was a part of a drinking crowd and who was well on the way to becoming an alcoholic. She eventually married him, and sadly, she and her children went through hell. Finally she went through a painful divorce and the loss of her home—her husband had drunk away all their assets. As she reflected on what had happened, she realized that all the pain was largely the result of her initial poor choice of friends.

One reason for the success of 12-Step programs is that they provide a way to build a new network with people who are not using drugs or alcohol.

One of the most reliable predictors of falling back into an addiction is the people you spend time with. If you hang out with people who drink, it is hard not to drink with them. If you hang out with people who use drugs, you will probably start using drugs again yourself.

What do you do if all your friends are involved in these activities? It may be a difficult choice, but making a clean break with the past may be the only way to a better future.

Everyone needs friends and people to interact with socially

each day—it is a basic human need. So if you need to leave your old social circle behind, it is important to develop a new one to replace it.

One of the reasons for the success of 12-Step programs is that they provide a way to build a new network with people who are not using drugs or alcohol. But there are other ways to build healthy social networks. Volunteer at your local animal shelter. Join a club. Get involved with sports or outdoor activities. Find a group of people with positive goals, and choose your new friends wisely.

Remember, you do have choices. If your habit is something that you do with a certain crowd, change your crowd. Get yourself out of that picture.

Feeling uncomfortable about answering questions about why you don't want to hang out with them anymore?

I well remember my father's advice one time when I was trying to end an unhealthy friendship. He looked me in the eye and said, "Neroli, you do not have to explain anything. You do not have to answer. You do not owe anyone an explanation. Just say no. Or smile and say nothing and walk away."

It was good advice, and it worked. I moved on, and that person soon forgot about me.

Forgiveness

AT ONE POINT IN OUR CONVERSATION I ASKED DANIEL IF he had forgiven his grandfather for getting him involved in pornography. He said that he had, and I was glad for him.

Forgiveness is freeing. When we forgive, we are forgiving the souls of those who may have caused us harm. This is easier to do when we realize that the point of light within their souls may also be trapped in habits or addictions or other burdens that cause them to act in ways that are harmful.

They may be victims of their lesser selves, the part of them that is not real—and yet commits unreality. This portion we leave to God and his angels. We can call for the arresting of the spirals of evil and ask the angels to remove the threads of darkness, the tares among the wheat. God says, "Vengeance is mine; I will repay." We can trust him to weigh all aspects of the situation in his own way and time, bringing divine justice to all, while we forgive the souls of those who may have harmed us.

> *Forgiveness is not just a nice thing to do. It is an essential part of healing.*

Forgiveness is not just a nice thing to do. It is an essential part of healing. When we withhold forgiveness from anyone, we are stopping the free flow of energy to and from our own heart, and in the end we are the ones who are hurt. People may have hurt us in the past, unwittingly or even intentionally, but if we can't forgive, our tie to them and their power over us continues. Some people define forgiveness as "giving up any hope for a better past." If we can forgive, we can be free.

The violet flame is also the mercy flame, and it can help to soften our heart so we are able to forgive. Do it for yourself, do it for another, do it for the part of God that lives within you both but is imprisoned until we forgive freely.

Forgiveness is the first step on the spiritual path, and it is often one of the first steps of healing. Remember that Jesus first forgave those whom he healed.

The following violet-flame mantra is specifically for forgiveness. As you give it, send beautiful violet-pink spheres to all you have wronged and all who have wronged you. Send them especially to those you have difficulty forgiving. And don't forget to forgive yourself.

FORGIVENESS

I AM forgiveness acting here,
Casting out all doubt and fear,
Setting men forever free
With wings of cosmic victory.

I AM calling in full power
For forgiveness every hour;
To all life in every place
I flood forth forgiving grace.

If you find it hard to forgive either yourself or another, do not forget the court of last resort in heaven, Kuan Yin. Give her mantras and feel her love and compassion enfolding you. Many have seen miracles of mercy and forgiveness from her blessed heart.

The Road to Recovery

SOME ADDICTION COUNSELORS WILL TELL YOU THAT THERE is a much better success rate when an addict or alcoholic is on probation or when his or her job is on the line. Others note that recovery is much harder for those who are on disability benefits, because they still get a check every month regardless of what they do with their lives. Many have been on welfare and addicted for so long that it is all that they know.

The hopeful side of these observations is that they reveal that the conscious mind has a lot of control over addiction—more than we might think. If we have something to live for, a purpose in life, this will help us summon the will to overcome the magnetism of addiction.

Some people find that point of will when they "hit bottom." The choice to live becomes very stark at that point, and they realize there is no longer any way to negotiate with their addiction. But it is not necessary to arrive at that place in order to summon the will to be free.

Addiction expert Stanton Peele tells the story of a man in his late sixties who had been smoking cigarettes since he was a teenager. When he awoke in a hospital bed after a heart attack, his first impulse was to reach for a cigarette. His daughter told him that if he touched another cigarette, she would never speak to him again. He quit on the spot and never smoked again. His love for his daughter provided the will that he needed to overcome his addiction.

But even when you find that thing that is worth living for,

this doesn't mean it is easy. Jenny described the early days of her recovery with these words: "You are just teetering on the edge. You are in the recovery program but you don't realize that you are just dry. At that point the self-esteem is so low that you don't feel worthy of being helped. This is of course not the case."

It is important to be realistic. Relapse is something that can occur at any time—even after twenty or thirty years of abstinence. Usually something triggers it—perhaps a stressful situation or a loss or sudden upset in life. For some people it has been a surgical operation for which they were given a prescription narcotic to deal with the pain. The use of the painkiller is a medical need initially, but then they remember that feeling and it is hard to stop when the medical need is no longer there.

Develop a support network, choose a healthy diet, get some form of exercise, and then choose any specific tools that fit your temperament and that you enjoy doing. And don't let up on your spiritual work.

In talking with former addicts about the possibility of relapse, many had a similar story to tell. They needed the support of a community of like-minded people who shared the same goals in order to make it. Many people find that support groups such as Alcoholics Anonymous are invaluable, even years after the acute phase of recovery.

They talk of the great value of having a structured program for recovery. Add to this whatever additional tools work for you: exercise, a healthy diet, supplements, journaling, yoga, tai chi, some form of meditation and mindfulness, or any of the other practices described here. All of these can be a great help, both short term and long term.

What is most important is that once you have chosen your program, work it consistently. At a minimum, include the basics: develop a support network, choose a healthy diet, get some form of exercise, and pursue some form of practice to expand your self-awareness. Choose the specific tools that fit your temperament and that you enjoy doing. If you enjoy them, it is easier to stay with them. And be consistent with your spiritual work.

Regardless of what else is happening in life, many people come a point where relapse is not an option anymore. They will do whatever it takes to have people and programs and tools in place that give them the best possible chance of succeeding.

Jenny advises those she is counselling through recovery:

Remember, recovery is a program of action. Working with a coach, a spiritual advisor, a sponsor—or sometimes all three—may be needed. Patiently strive for improvement. Daily discipline is essential.

Learn to live one day at a time. That anxious apartness that so many experience every day will, as time passes, no longer control your life—if you constructively learn new behaviors and disciplines. The violet flame is the most powerful tool on earth for this kind of transformation. With God all things are possible, and it is indeed possible to move that mountain.

PART 8

12 STEPS TO FREEDOM

12-Step Programs

ALCOHOLICS ANONYMOUS AND ITS OFFSHOOTS HAVE assisted many people on the path to recovery through their 12-Step programs. Although the AA path is not for everyone, these programs have been an irreplaceable lifeline for many. The 12 Steps are simple but powerful. Here is the original version published by Alcoholics Anonymous:

1. We admitted we were powerless over alcohol—that our lives had become unmanageable.
2. Came to believe that a power greater than ourselves could restore us to sanity.
3. Made a decision to turn our will and our lives over to the care of God *as we understood Him.*
4. Made a searching and fearless moral inventory of ourselves.
5. Admitted to God, to ourselves, and to another human being the exact nature of our wrongs.
6. Were entirely ready to have God remove all these defects of character.
7. Humbly asked Him to remove our shortcomings.
8. Made a list of all persons we had harmed, and became willing to make amends to them all.
9. Made direct amends to such people wherever possible, except when to do so would injure them or others.
10. Continued to take personal inventory, and when we were wrong, promptly admitted it.
11. Sought through prayer and meditation to improve our con-

scious contact with God *as we understood Him*, praying only for knowledge of His will for us and the power to carry that out.

12. Having had a spiritual awakening as the result of these steps, we tried to carry this message to alcoholics, and to practice these principles in all our affairs.

Each of the 12 Steps can also be reduced further to one word:

Step 1	Honesty
Step 2	Hope
Step 3	Faith
Step 4	Courage
Step 5	Integrity
Step 6	Willingness
Step 7	Humility
Step 8	Brotherly Love
Step 9	Justice
Step 10	Perseverance
Step 11	Spiritual
Step 12	Service

If you lean towards Buddhism, consider the 12 Steps as they are described by Darren Littlejohn in *The 12-Step Buddhist*:

Step 1	Acceptance
Step 2	Confidence
Step 3	Surrender
Step 4	Self-Examination
Step 5	Self-Honesty
Step 6	Willingness
Step 7	Humility
Step 8	Forgiveness
Step 9	Restitution
Step 10	Admission
Step 11	Seeking
Step 12	Unconditional Love

The 12 Steps and the Spiritual Path

A S I READ THE 12 STEPS I AM STRUCK BY THE DEEP spirituality at their core. The steps continually turn you back to reliance on a higher power. In the process of recovery through the 12 Steps, many do go back to their former religions; others explore new spiritual paths and traditions.

Jenny shared with me this perspective on addiction and religion: "It is said that in religion we believe we are going to hell. But real spirituality is for people who have already been there—because addiction is a hell of our own making, even though we may not realize it for a considerable time."

If you're an addict like me, you have a choice: a spiritual way of life or addiction.
—DARREN LITTLEJOHN

Darren Littlejohn, author of *The 12-Step Buddhist*, says, "If you're an addict like me, you have a choice: a spiritual way of life or addiction."

I find that more and more people are looking for universal paths that are not confined to any one religion. The teachings of the ascended masters incorporate many spiritual paths, embracing the truth from all the world's religions, including Christianity, Kabbalah, Hinduism and Buddhism. The masters' teachings also give a new meaning to the 12 Steps.

With Jenny's help, I have taken the 12 Steps and integrated prayers and mantras to complement each step. Jenny believes that these non-denominational affirmations can bring people through the storm more quickly. This version of the 12 Steps is from AA, so it uses the terms specific to alcohol, but the same principles apply equally to any addiction.

12 Steps with the Ascended Masters

Step 1 We admitted we were powerless over alcohol—that our lives had become unmanageable.

The first step is *Honesty*—admitting that you have a problem. Jenny says, "Your life becomes unmanageable when using a substance to medicate your pain no longer works. It is a wonder that people survive the panic attacks and the anxiety that often come at this stage. Just giving the simple mantra 'I AM a being of violet fire! I AM the purity God desires!' will calm the mind."

People dealing with addiction are typically restless, irritable and discontented, prey to anxiety and depression. In order to counter this, the mind needs to concentrate on something that it can hang on to. This is one reason why a simple mantra is helpful in the first stages of recovery. The more you focus on a single decree like this with conviction, the more quickly the panic attacks will subside.

I AM a being of violet fire!
I AM the purity God desires!

It can be said over and over again until calm descends and peace of mind is restored. Even when you have been free from your addiction for some time, you may find that a lot of stuff will come up—just the circumstances or challenges in life—that can put you back in a place where you feel that things are out of control. That is the time to return once more to the basics.

Jenny explains, "This simple two line mantra can be a life

saver. It is the simplest decree to memorize and say. Should you be severely disturbed, write it out a hundred times, if need be, and repeat it every time out loud—or just keep saying it. Keep a violet-flame wallet card with this mantra on your desk or in your car. The more often you use it, the sooner you will find that once the mind is calm, you are able to take action."

Here is a longer version of the mantra:

LIGHT, SET ME FREE!

Light, set me free! Light, set me free!
    Light, set me free!
Light command, Light command,
    Light command, command, command!
Light demand, Light demand,
    Light demand, demand, demand!
Light expand, Light expand,
    Light expand, expand, expand!
Light I AM, Light I AM,
    Light I AM, I AM, I AM!
I AM a being of violet fire,
I AM the purity God desires!

Step 2 We came to believe that a power greater than
ourselves could restore us to sanity.

This second step is *Hope.* Jenny explains, "This is the step where you finally realize that there has to be a higher power. You find that the drugs and the alcohol have such a huge control over you that you have to find a God of your understanding which is greater than this toxic substance that has become your god."

Your real hope is in your Higher Self, which is the power that is greater than yourself that you always have access to. The Higher Self is diagrammed in the Chart of Your Divine Self (see page 34).

You have a mighty I AM Presence above you. Your Holy Christ Self is the voice within that tells you right from wrong and which way to go. Unfortunately, this voice of conscience is one that many people ignore. Listening to that voice and following its lead is a key to overcoming the darkness that is trying to overtake you.

The "Tube of Light" mantra calls for a shimmering waterfall of light all around you, a beautiful and powerful forcefield of protection that can help you to attune to that inner voice and shield you against the "other voices"—those that would try to bring you down.

TUBE OF LIGHT

> Beloved I AM Presence bright,
> Round me seal your tube of light
> From ascended master flame
> Called forth now in God's own name.
> Let it keep my temple free
> From all discord sent to me.
>
> I AM calling forth violet fire
> To blaze and transmute all desire,
> Keeping on in freedom's name
> Till I AM one with the violet flame.

Step 3 *We made a decision to turn our will and our lives over to the care of God* as we understood Him.

Step 3 is the step of *Faith*, turning ourselves over to the will of God. Sometimes people hesitate to take this step. They are afraid that the will of God might be some sort of straightjacket, that there would be no joy in a life lived in the will of God.

But actually, the will of God for us is the realization of our true nature, our inner blueprint, our real purpose in life, and fulfilling these things is the greatest source of lasting joy. Suffering is the result when we are out of alignment with this inner being.

The will of God is a blue sphere above you right now, and there are mantras that can help you to access that will of God. Visualize it as a blue sphere forming around you as you give the mantras to call forth God's will into your life.

Give the Third-Step prayer from Alcoholics Anonymous followed by the mantras for the will of God in multiples of three.

THIRD-STEP PRAYER

God, I offer myself to Thee—to build with me and to do with me as Thou wilt. Relieve me of the bondage of self, that I may better do Thy will. Take away my difficulties, that victory over them may bear witness to those I would help, of Thy Power, Thy Love and Thy Way of Life. May I do Thy will always!

MANTRAS FOR THE WILL OF GOD

**Not My Will, Not My Will, Not My Will
but Thine Be Done!**

The Will of God is Good!

Thy Will, O God, is Good. Alleluia Amen!

Lo! I AM Come to Do Thy Will, O God!

Once we make the decision to turn our lives over to God, he can send his angels and archangels to help us. Almost everyone loves angels, and their greatest desire is to help us. But they must have our call to be able to intercede. Archangel Michael, the captain of the hosts of the Lord, can be your best friend. Get to know him, call to him, he will be right there at your side.

ARCHANGEL MICHAEL'S MANTRA FOR PROTECTION

> Lord Michael before,
> Lord Michael behind,
> Lord Michael to the right,
> Lord Michael to the left,
> Lord Michael above,
> Lord Michael below,
> Lord Michael, Lord Michael wherever I go!
> *I AM his love protecting here! (3x)

You can also use the decree "Lord Michael," on page 100, to call for Archangel Michael's presence with you.

Step 4 *We made a searching and fearless moral inventory of ourselves.*

Step 4 is *Courage*. And it does take courage to make a searching personal inventory if your life has been seriously off track. Socrates said that the unexamined life is not worth living. But in order for you to begin a fearless moral inventory, which many of us have never, ever done, a humble belief in a power greater than yourself is required. Without this point of reality and hope for change, it can be overwhelming to examine one's failings.

When faced with fear of what you might find when you look within, try this mantra. The color of fearlessness is a brilliant white light tinged with a beautiful emerald green. As you give this mantra, see that brilliant white and emerald light dissolving the fear, replacing it with fearlessness. Repeat this mantra as often as necessary in multiples of three. (This mantra is also used to bring spiritual and material abundance.)

MANTRA FOR OVERCOMING FEAR

> I AM free from fear and doubt,
> Casting want and misery out,

Knowing now all good Supply
Ever comes from realms on high.

I AM the hand of God's own Fortune
Flooding forth the treasures of Light,
Now receiving full Abundance
To supply each need of Life.

Another mantra for overcoming fear is the one that is known as the spiritual SOS! All the angels know it. When the angels hear it, they know you need help, you are serious, and you mean business. This mantra says in essence, "I need help and I need it now!" Shout it out loud in the face of all doubts and fears, all that would stand in the way of your freedom.

THE LIGHT OF GOD NEVER FAILS!

The Light of God never fails!
The Light of God never fails!
The Light of God never fails!
And the Beloved Mighty I AM Presence is that Light!

As you go through your fearless inventory, also include a realistic assessment of your strengths and positive qualities. Don't minimize or discount these—they are the positive momentums you can build on to overcome the negatives. Even if they only appear from time to time at this stage, they are aspects of your Higher Self that you can nurture and grow until they become the predominant qualities in your life.

Step 5   We admitted to God, to ourselves, and to another human being the exact nature of our wrongs.

Step 5 is *Integrity*. Admitting to our wrongs is a very important step, a key to making the concrete changes that we need in our life.

The ritual of confession has a long history in Christianity as a means of reconciling the soul with God. In Catholic tradition, confession is made to a priest. In Protestant traditions, confession is usually made to God alone. But this ritual did not begin with Christianity—Gautama Buddha taught it to his disciples.

The ritual of confession is powerful because it allows us to put distance between ourselves and the wrongs we have done. It allows us to look at them objectively, acknowledge they are there, and also to realize that they don't define who we are as a soul.

Our wrongs, when they are not surrendered, become a heavy burden. When we confess them, we are letting them go, no longer holding on to them. When we have confessed our wrongs, then we can accept forgiveness—from God and man.

Give the following mantra, which affirms forgiveness. Give it every day and feel that light of forgiveness lifting your burdens. And as you are doing this, also send forgiveness to all others in your life, especially those you have had difficulty with.

FORGIVENESS

I AM forgiveness acting here,
Casting out all doubt and fear,
Setting men forever free
With wings of cosmic victory.

I AM calling in full power
For forgiveness every hour;
To all life in every place
I flood forth forgiving grace.

Step 6 *We were entirely ready to have God remove all these defects of character.*

This step is about *Willingness*. Jenny says that this step "separates the men from the boys." This is where we really decide that we want to change.

Jenny counsels those in the grips of addiction to ask, "What

is it costing me when I carry out this negative addictive behavior?" She says that if you are honest you will see "it is costing
me everything—my life, my peace of mind, my family, my work,
my relationships, and on and on."

Our defects of character are like outworn garments. Sometimes we have a favorite old sweater that may have a few holes,
but because it is familiar and comfortable, it is hard to let it go.
In the same way, it is sometimes hard to let go of our defects
simply because we are used to them, and perhaps we don't know
how to function without them. But until we let them go, we don't
make the space for something better to replace them.

As you use the "Transfiguration" mantra, see yourself putting
off these old garments, putting on in their place the garments of
your Higher Self.

TRANSFIGURATION

I AM changing all my garments,
Old ones for the bright new day;
With the sun of understanding
I AM shining all the way.

I AM light within, without;
I AM light is all about.
Fill me, free me, glorify me!
Seal me, heal me, purify me!
Until transfigured they describe me:
I AM shining like the Son,
I AM shining like the Sun! (3x)

Step 7 We humbly asked Him to remove our shortcomings.

Humility is the essence of Step 7. Sometimes we find that it
is the repeated humiliations of addiction that force us to learn
something of humility. Here is the Seventh-Step Prayer from
Alcoholics Anonymous.

SEVENTH-STEP PRAYER

My Creator, I am now willing that you should have all of me, good and bad. I pray that you now remove from me every single defect of character which stands in the way of my usefulness to you and my fellows. Grant me strength, as I go out from here, to do your bidding. Amen.

This prayer is a good beginning. But to take it further we need to understand that if we could remove our own short-comings we would not need God to remove them from us. Part of the problem is that these defects are deeply engrained in us. For many of us, they were the mechanisms we used as children to cope with situations where we were subject to dysfunctional adults. They may have enabled us to survive in very difficult circumstances, but they no longer serve us well.

The more we focus on our defects the bigger they get. Instead, we need to erase them with the cosmic eraser, the violet trans-muting flame. Once we have done that, we replace them with positive momentums we want to build. We can do this with the resurrection flame, an energy that restores life and wholeness.

The resurrection flame is a powerful cleanser, purifier and healer. Call it forth with this "Resurrection" mantra.

RESURRECTION

I AM the Flame of Resurrection
Blazing God's pure Light through me.
Now I AM raising every atom,
From every shadow I AM free.

I AM the Light of God's full Presence,
I AM living ever free.
Now the flame of Life eternal
Rises up to Victory.

*Step 8   We made a list of all persons we had harmed, and
          became willing to make amends to them all.*

Step 8 is all about *Brotherly Love*. You take the practical step of
making a list of all persons that you have harmed. Don't go rush-
ing out to make amends yet—just concentrate on making your
list. Each situation must be carefully looked at. How have you
harmed that person? In what way?

As you write your list, expand the flame of love in your heart
by giving this mantra from Saint Germain. Send that love to all
those on your list, to all you have ever wronged and to all who
have ever wronged you.

I AM THE LIGHT OF THE HEART
by Saint Germain

I AM the Light of the Heart
Shining in the darkness of being
And changing all into the golden treasury
Of the Mind of Christ.

I AM projecting my Love
Out into the world
To erase all errors
And to break down all barriers.

I AM the power of infinite Love,
Amplifying itself
Until it is victorious,
World without end!

*Step 9   We made direct amends to such people wherever
          possible, except when to do so would injure them
          or others.*

Step 9 is all about *Justice*—not man's justice but God's justice.
Now that you have your list from Step 8 of all the people you

have harmed, think about how you could make amends.

Amends can be a sincere apology, financial remuneration, fulfilling emotional needs, amends to your employer for not being the best employee that you could have been, service of some kind, replacing a stolen object, and so on. Think about each person individually and what could help them to be made whole from the harm you have done them.

There must be a complete readiness on your behalf to make amends when the opportunity arises. You make amends except when to do so will cause harm to others.

You make amends to others with service and love. Remember that it doesn't help to point out to others any negative behavior on their part—even if you think this may have contributed to your behavior. Do not in any way accuse or blame others. Simply take responsibility for your own actions. You can then live in this world and be free.

If it should happen the amends that you offer are not received, just accept that fact, even though it might hurt you deeply. And even if they don't want to receive anything physically, you can continue to pray for them. You can also place a photograph somewhere you will see it regularly and just send them a blessing each time you pass by. Wish that person every good thing. Don't go back, don't live in the past, just move on in prayer and peace. They may have a change of heart in time.

In some cases you may have no idea where the person is. Some of them may have even made their transition to other worlds. You may not be able to serve these people physically, but you can still lift their burdens spiritually by sending them the violet flame. Visualize spheres of violet flame with wings on either side, winging their way to each person—wherever they are in whatever octave. The violet flame has its own innate intelligence. It knows where to go—wherever that one is.

When you do seek to make amends to others, remember that

the most important ingredient of your service is the love you put into it. Next comes the wisdom to know how best to express that love. Finally there is the action that makes that love and wisdom tangible. The following mantras can help you to endow all of this with the violet flame.

HEART

Violet Fire, thou Love divine,
Blaze within this heart of mine!
Thou art Mercy forever true,
Keep me always in tune with you.

HEAD

I AM Light, thou Christ in me,
Set my mind forever free;
Violet Fire, forever shine
Deep within this mind of mine.

God who gives my daily bread,
With Violet Fire fill my head
Till thy radiance heavenlike
Makes my mind a mind of Light.

HAND

I AM the hand of God in action,
Gaining Victory every day;
My pure soul's great satisfaction
Is to walk the Middle Way.

Step 10 We continued to take personal inventory, and when we were wrong, promptly admitted it.

Step 10 is *Perseverance*. We continue on. We continue to self-assess and take personal inventory. In this step we are committing to remain anchored in reality—no longer allowing ourselves to pretend things are OK when they are not. A period of reflection each day in journaling can be a way to keep this commitment that carries many additional benefits. The following mantra can help us to maintain that inner sense of direction in life.

GOD DIRECTION

> I AM life of God direction
> Blaze thy light of truth in me,
> Focus here all God's perfection
> From all discord set me free
>
> Make and keep me anchored ever
> In the justice of thy plan,
> I AM the presence of perfection
> Living the life of God in man.

It is also important to call to the angels to help us, to deal with all the unseen forces that would try to take us away from that commitment. We deal with these forces on a daily basis—the cause behind the effect of addiction—and for this we need the powerful presence of Michael, Prince of the Archangels.

Pope Leo's Prayer to Archangel Michael is one of the most powerful prayers of exorcism of the forces of addiction and the dark forces that attack our families. Miracles have been wrought with this simple prayer.

Give it nine times or more each day. It is good to give it early in the morning, before anyone in your family has started their day. It will seal the place where evil dwells and cut you and your family free from the unseen forces that move against you.

POPE LEO'S PRAYER TO ARCHANGEL MICHAEL

Saint Michael the Archangel, defend us in Armageddon. Be our protection against the wickedness and snares of the devil. May God rebuke him, we humbly pray. And

do thou, O Prince of the heavenly host, by the power of God, bind the forces of Death and Hell, the seed of Satan, the false hierarchy of Antichrist, and all evil spirits who wander through the world for the ruin of souls, and remand them to the Court of the Sacred Fire for their Final Judgment [including _____].*

Cast out the dark ones and their darkness, the evildoers and their evil words and works, cause, effect, record and memory, into the lake of sacred fire "prepared for the devil and his angels."

In the name of the Father, the Son, the Holy Spirit and the Mother, Amen.

Step 11 We sought through prayer and meditation to improve our conscious contact with God as we understood Him, praying only for knowledge of His will for us and the power to carry that out.

Step 11 is summarized in the word *Spiritual*. Prayer and meditation are vital components in recovery. All addiction is a soul sickness: prayer and meditation are the medicine. Just as we need food and water to nurture our body, so we need prayer and meditation to nurture our spirit.

In prayer, man makes intercession to God for assistance. In meditation, he gives assistance to God by creating the nature of God within his own thoughts and feelings.

The Prayer of Saint Francis has been a comfort to many in recovery. It brings great peace as well as a shift of focus. Instead of dwelling in our own problems and burdens, it encourages us to think about others and how we can help them in their need. It gives a vision of what life can be beyond addiction.

---

* On the first repetition of this prayer, name here the unseen forces behind the addiction. Then repeat the prayer without this insert.

PRAYER OF SAINT FRANCIS

Lord,

Make me an instrument of thy peace.
Where there is hatred let me sow love;
Where there is injury, pardon;
Where there is doubt, faith;
Where there is despair, hope;
Where there is darkness, light; and
Where there is sadness, joy.

O Divine Master,

Grant that I may not so much
Seek to be consoled as to console;
To be understood as to understand;
To be loved as to love.
For it is in giving that we receive,
It is in pardoning that we are pardoned, and
It is in dying that we are born to eternal Life.

What is it that dies? The Real Self does not die. It is the lesser self, the not-self, the enemy within, that dies. We must be willing to let the old, negative self go so that the Real Self can be born within us. The Prayer of Saint Francis can help us make that surrender each day.

Step 12 Having had a spiritual awakening as the result
of these steps, we tried to carry this message to
alcoholics, and to practice these principles in
all our affairs.

Service is the key in this final step. You seal the victories of the previous steps by sharing them with others. In serving others you forget your own concerns and you reinforce your own path to freedom. The joy of living is the theme of the 12 Steps, and the greatest joy is often found in service.

175

The decree "I AM Light" is Jenny's favorite violet-flame decree. The first time she gave it she felt an immediate response and a sense of comfort and peace. Jenny told me: "Even though I was a licensed therapist and counselor, helping others to heal from addiction, it was not until I learned to invoke the violet flame that I really understood that this spiritual tool had been the missing link in my own life. Even though I sponsored many people and I did service work, it did not always quiet the ceaseless yearning inside. Finding the violet flame and actually sitting down and doing it was the key. When I used the violet flame I found that the gnawing anxiety could not remain inside me.

"At first there was great resistance within me to using the violet flame. Addicts and alcoholics are often movers and shakers and we do not want to sit still. But I was willing to go outside my comfort zone and give some simple violet flame decrees. This has made all the difference in my life."

The walk through the 12 Steps is a journey from darkness to light. In Step 12, we share that light with others to help them in their journeys. "The I AM Light" decree is a beautiful thought-form for sharing the light with all we meet.

I AM LIGHT
by Kuthumi

I AM light, glowing light,
Radiating light, intensified light.
God consumes my darkness,
Transmuting it into light.

This day I AM a focus of the Central Sun.
Flowing through me is a crystal river,
A living fountain of light
That can never be qualified
By human thought and feeling.
I AM an outpost of the Divine.

Such darkness as has used me is swallowed up
By the mighty river of light which I AM.

I AM, I AM, I AM light;
I live, I live, I live in light.
I AM light's fullest dimension;
I AM light's purest intention.
I AM light, light, light
Flooding the world everywhere I move,
Blessing, strengthening and conveying
The purpose of the kingdom of heaven.

We can also affirm in this step the goal of life, our ultimate and final freedom not only from addiction but also from all of the burdens of earthly life. As you give this decree, see the white light of the ascension flame all around you.

ASCENSION

I AM Ascension Light,
Victory flowing free,
All of Good won at last
For all eternity.

I AM Light, all weights are gone.
Into the air I raise;
To all I pour with full God Power
My wondrous song of praise.

All hail! I AM the living Christ,
The ever-loving One.
Ascended now with full God Power,
I AM a blazing Sun!

The Goal of Life

FOR MANY PEOPLE, ADDICTION IS THE HARDEST LIFE-LESSON they will face. Many people say it is so hard because they have an inability to be rigorously honest.

Being honest does not mean condemning yourself for what you have done. It has nothing to do with blame. It means to look at your life squarely, the good and the bad. This is the core principle of the physical, behavioral, psychological and spiritual changes that are spoken of in *The Big Book* of Alcoholics Anonymous and that can be realized by working the steps.

As she has walked her own journey through recovery, Jenny Hunter has helped many people deal with addiction of all kinds. She says, "We have a saying in AA, 'We don't shoot our wounded.' This is simple statement, but it has a profound meaning. The process of recovery begins with acknowledging our wounds. Then we learn that our wounds will only heal if we have the courage to look at them instead of repeatedly rubbing salt in them by affirming how bad we feel."

She asserts that it all begins with the mind. Some people estimate that we have approximately 60,000 thoughts each day. In addicts and alcoholics most of these thoughts are negative—in fact, addicts are addicted to negativity and negative thoughts as much as anything. Jenny says, "Everything about the addiction is negative. It is not possible to be addicted to any substance without the corresponding negative thought process. In recovery we learn to substitute positive thinking for the negative thinking."

You will find as you continue on the journey of recovery that the more that you focus on where you are going and what you want to manifest in your life, the better off you will be. Rather than continually affirming how bad your life and circumstances are, concentrate on the positive aspects that you wish to manifest. Affirm that these are *already appearing*. Jenny reminds her clients, "I only see greatness for you." As we hold this vision for ourselves, it will be more and more real day by day.

She tells them to use the steps in the order that they have been given and to work with a sponsor who understands them and is a fine example of someone who is living them.

Jenny says, "Those of you have been in recovery for a long time know that you still struggle within yourself every day. There is a way out, and it is simple. The violet flame is a part of the solution. If you are truly ready to take this journey of uncovering what is buried within you, discovering your real self, and discarding that which no longer serves you, then you can achieve a life beyond your wildest dreams."

> *If you are truly ready to take this journey of uncovering what is buried within you, discovering your real self, and discarding that which no longer serves you, then you can achieve a life beyond your wildest dreams.*
>
> —JENNY

PART 9

WANTING TO BE FREE

A New Life

FOR MANY PEOPLE, ONE OF THE MAJOR CHALLENGES IN overcoming addiction is building a new life. Many addicts have a group of friends and a social network whose connection centers around the addiction. Once you determine to leave it behind, even when you have found your initial freedom from the addiction, what will your life look like? Who can you turn to if you lose your job or you need a place to stay or in some other emergency? And what will you do every day after work and on weekends?

Friends and social interaction are a basic human need—we all have a need to connect with other people with whom we have common interests. What do you do when all your friends are in the scene you are trying to leave?

This is especially challenging in recovery from alcohol, because alcohol is part of the social life of such a high percentage of people today. They may be fine drinking moderately (or even to excess occasionally) on social occasions, but if you are a recovering alcoholic, it is very dangerous to put yourself in a situation where there is the pressure or the temptation to have "just one drink." The problem is now becoming more challenging for those trying to overcome an addiction to marijuana, as recreational use of the drug is being made legal in more places and its use is becoming more widespread and socially acceptable.

For those in the initial stages of recovery (or for those who have had an issue in the past with relapses), a halfway house may be a key step. These facilities provide a safe, structured environ-

ment, strong peer support and often counselling and other services to ease the transition to living independently.

Beyond this, one of the most important services that AA/NA
groups provide is a network of people with a common interest in
living free from addiction. Some of these groups organize social
activities for members outside of the formal recovery meetings,
and even those that don't can provide a connection point for
sober activities in your area.

There are also many groups that provide social and other
activities specifically for those seeking to live a sober lifestyle.
Some are groups organized specifically for those in recovery, such
as Phoenix Multisport. Others are formal or informal groups providing alcohol-free social activities for those who want to abstain
or even those who just want to participate in alcohol-free events
occasionally. Meetup.com lists hundreds of groups for those who
want to get together for drug- and alcohol-free social events and
hundreds more groups specifically for support and recovery.
Many others can readily be found through web searches

You may wonder what your life will be like without your
addiction, how you will spend your time. Sometimes it is simply a
matter of faith, following your inner promptings, and taking the
opportunities that God sends your way.

Family Patterns

ONE OF THE BIGGEST CHALLENGES IN RECOVERING FROM addiction is that once you are free from the immediate effects of the drug, you will have to deal once more with the mental and emotional pain that you had sought to escape through chemical means.

This may not be an easy task—if it had been easy, you might have found a better way to deal with it the first time around. However, with greater insight and better strategies, it is possible to chart a new course, and in the process, find deep healing and spiritual growth.

One avenue that many in recovery have pursued is to look at patterns of addiction in their family. Many people who have been challenged by addiction have had one or both parents who also had issues with alcohol or drugs, and they have found great benefit from working with the concepts of those who have written about adult children of alcoholics.

A book by Janet Woititz, *Adult Children of Alcoholics,* was the first to bring this issue to public awareness. Without any promotion or advertising, it made the *New York Times* bestseller list in 1987 and stayed there for almost a year. Many people would read it and for the first time feel that they understood their childhood and themselves as adults. Then they would give copies to all their family members, wanting to share their insights.

The central premise of the book is that children who grow up in a family where alcoholism is an issue don't learn what other children learn. They develop wonderful strengths in surviving crises, but don't learn the day-to-day patterns of leading a normal, stable life. The same is also true for children growing up in families where dysfunction and chaos are caused by factors other than alcohol, including gambling problems, sexual abuse, drug use or mental illness.

If your childhood had elements of this kind of chaos and uncertainty, from whatever cause, you may find that simply reading books for children of alcoholics can be healing. As you gain insight into the patterns in your life and the missing elements in personality development, you can gain a level of peace about them through understanding their point of origin. Realizing that they are not inherent defects in your soul but simply a function of your environment, you know also that they can be healed.

Since Woititz's groundbreaking book was first published, many others have explored its themes further, and there are a number of workbooks that provide very practical exercises for developing missing life skills. There are also many counsellors who have specific training in helping adult children of alcoholics. Professional counselling is especially valuable for those who have faced sexual abuse in childhood, since the wounds from this go very deep in the psyche. There are also many support groups for survivors of these experiences who find strength in walking through their healing journeys together.

There is a saying in the Bible about the sins of the fathers being visited on their children to the third and fourth generation. This is nowhere more clear than in the case of alcoholism and sexual abuse, which often run for generations through families.

But the Bible also says, "I will remember their sins no more." Healing is possible and the cycle can be broken. The karmic burdens can be transmuted with the violet flame, and new patterns can be built in the psyche. We can find freedom from the burdens of our family tree.

The Re-Creation of Self

A KEY ELEMENT OF WORKING WITH MINDFULNESS AND psychology is that these approaches are both designed to bring the elements of the subconscious into conscious awareness. If we are not aware of them, they can control much of our behavior as we are tossed on the sea of emotions, without our even knowing how or why. If we make these patterns conscious, they no longer have the same power over us.

Neuroscientists are now discovering the inner workings of brain chemistry that explain how this works on a cellular level, but it is not necessary to know all those details in order to experience what the saints and mystics have known for thousands of years: that with conscious awareness of what is happening within, we gain the ability to choose what path we will take. We find that we can create new patterns to replace the old ones that no longer serve us well.

This re-creation of self may not be an easy process. We didn't create who we are in a day, and we can't recreate ourselves in a day. We may have setbacks. But if we do, it is important not to see these as signs of failure, but as new opportunities for learning. Observe what happened, your thoughts and feelings, and learn from the experience.

This transformative process of finding freedom can be greatly accelerated by regular spiritual practice—something else the mystics have known for thousands of years. We have covered spiritual techniques in some detail in Part 6, and in addiction perhaps the most important initially is the work of protection and cutting oneself free from the entities of addiction, those astral forces which can have such a powerful influence on one's mental and emotional state if they are allowed to remain.

The other vital spiritual tool is the use of the violet flame to clear the records of addiction and heal the damage to the finer bodies and the physical body. The violet flame also penetrates the subconscious and unconscious mind, transmuting negative patterns and momentums, freeing up tremendous quantities of energy that can now flow into positive patterns of our choosing.

Beyond 12 Steps

THERE IS NO DOUBT THAT MILLIONS OF PEOPLE HAVE OVER-come addictions through 12-Step programs. But there are some people who are looking for even more. They want to get beyond the traditional affirmation that people use to introduce themselves at AA meetings, "I am an alcoholic," or "I am a recovering alcoholic."

They have gone through a 12-Step program or some other means of overcoming their addiction and they have a solid foundation of abstinence. Now they are looking to remake themselves, to no longer have their addiction or their former self define who they are.

People are saying, "I am not an addict and I am not my addiction. I

> *We must become the perfect child of God, the son or daughter of God that has always been inside of us. I have found that with the violet flame we can do exactly that.*
>
> —JENNY

am a valuable human being and I have a mission and a purpose." They accept themselves as spiritual beings with a temporary problem. In spiritual terms, we could say that they want to identify with their Higher Self rather than their addiction—and the addiction is no part of that Higher Self.

This is a process of recreating our mental and emotional states. As we transform self-defeating patterns of old thoughts and feelings, we come to the place where we can literally remake ourselves after the image of our Real Self, our authentic self. The violet flame is a key element of this, since it can dissolve the momentums and of the past. But we also have to change so that we don't recreate them, if only because this is the only way we know how to be.

Remaking oneself in this way is not easy. It has been likened to the "mighty work of the ages." It is work, and it does require a willingness to go to the depths of one's being, a willingness to experience the pain that was suppressed in the past.

When it comes up again, the pain may at first seem overwhelming, the pull to slip backwards may seem irresistible. At times like this the urge to find some quick way out may loom very large. Sometimes distraction can be a good strategy—watch a movie, go for a run, something to take your mind in a different direction.

But eventually you will find that if you just sit with the feeling—allow yourself to feel it, observe it, name it, describe it, perhaps write about it in your journal—the intensity will subside. You will find that you are more than the feeling, and you will come through to the other side. You will find that you have a power in you that is greater than addiction and you are becoming more of your Real Self. And the angels will reinforce that power and determination when you call for their help.

But even when you have worked through the recreation of self, it is not a sign that your victory is secure and that you can let down your guard. Jesus himself spoke of the danger of allowing entities to come back into one's house after they have been cast out.

Vigilance and spiritual protection are necessary as long as we live in a world where the forces of darkness behind addiction are so prevalent.

Other Gods

THE FIRST OF THE TEN COMMANDMENTS SAYS, "THOU shalt have no other gods before me." It is easy to accept this in principle. We don't make sacrifices at pagan altars. We may even go to church. Yet many of us have unwittingly created our own "gods" in more subtle ways.

It has been said that our creator is a jealous God, which means that God wants to have all of us. He created us, even the physical bodies that we wear, and ultimately we belong to him. We have many human relationships in life, but our relationship with God, our Source, should be the primary one. Perhaps in a broad sense, addiction could be defined as anything that takes us from our love of God.

Daniel and I talked about the fact that you can be addicted to or obsessed with anything—work, food, sex, television, a person, an animal, an object or thing, a practice or a habit. If there is anything in your world that is more important to you than your relationship with God, this becomes your "god."

In this sense, we may all have elements of addiction to various degrees. We may not have the kind of addiction that prevents us from functioning within the norms of life and society. We may even be very successful in worldly terms. But if we find that there are habits and momentums that from time to time undermine our highest goals, what we really want to be and do, that separate us from the love of God and those around us even in small ways, then we have work to do.

The spiritual tools in this book are presented in the context of addictions that are more obvious and more overtly harmful, such as drugs, alcohol and pornography. But they can also help us find freedom from other more subtle negative conditions, such as anger, fear or pride. Any of these can also be a block to our freedom to fulfill our highest destiny and purpose in life.

That ultimate freedom to walk the spiritual path, by any name, can lead us back to the prefect love that we all once knew, when we and our twin flame were first formed in that point of light in the heart of God.

True Freedom

I WAS GLAD THAT GOD HAD PLACED ME IN THE SEAT NEXT TO Daniel on that flight and that we had the chance to share so much. I was grateful that he had the courage to tell me about himself and to allow me to share with him some of the concepts I have shared in this book. I know that his story reflects the path of any of us who has grappled with addiction. As we disembarked from the plane and said our goodbyes outside the gate, I wished him well and prayed that the angels would continue to be with him.

Daniel's story gives hope that no matter the source of an addiction, no matter how long we may have been caught up in it, we can overcome. I hope that this book has given you insights into the world of addiction and the keys to overcoming.

Daniel told me, "I got what I wanted. I prayed and He sent help. It wasn't the way that I expected it, but it worked."

Wanting to be free—the want is the impetus that drives everything else. Daniel had that want, an intense desire to be free.

I believe that we all have that impulse within us. The soul of every man, woman and child wants to be free. Sometimes other desires cloud the inner calling of the soul—an outer need, a temporary pleasure, a desire to avoid pain or responsibility. Sometimes it is just the aggressive energies of unseen forces.

But beyond all this, your soul wants freedom, at all levels of being. And I fully believe that you can obtain it. Please know that my prayers go with you as you find the courage within to seek true freedom.

PART 10

SEVEN KEYS TO OVERCOME ADDICTION

NEAR THE END OF MY CONVERSATION WITH DANIEL, as the plane was starting its descent into Salt Lake City, I began to make a list of some of the keys we were uncovering. I also reflected on having watched others overcome their addictions.

Here are some simple but helpful keys from the trenches.

1. Work on the problem at all levels

At its core, addiction is a spiritual problem. But it also has mental, emotional and often physical components. To be most effective, work on the problem at all these levels.

2. Outsmart the not-self

Daniel told me that in reordering his life, he could no longer own a computer or use the Internet. He felt that his habit was so deeply ingrained that the temptation to indulge again would be too great, and it was not worth the risk to him.

That was quite a decision to make in the Information Age. But Daniel knew himself—he showed insight and common sense, and he knew what he needed to do for his victory.

Such a decision might not be necessary for everyone dealing with his addiction. But what can be learned from his example is that you need to know yourself and work out whatever strategy is necessary to outsmart your addiction.

If your habit is something that you do in private, go to a public setting when you are tempted. If you have a drinking problem, don't keep alcohol in the house. Know your limitations and do not expect from yourself what you know you cannot give. Set boundaries for yourself that you know will be safe and that will prevent you from getting in a situation where you might make a decision you would later regret.

3. Enlist the help of others

Daniel was fortunate that he had a good support system—a family who loved him and stood by him and a community who knew how to pray. He let people know what he was wrestling with, and he found that many came forward to help him through the challenges.

Asking for help is an important step in moving on from addiction. Some people don't ask for help because they are worried that friends or colleagues will reject them or look down upon them. But more often than not, people are very willing to help if you are sincere in wanting to overcome addiction. The benefit from the support of loving souls who understand is invaluable.

4. Choose the company you keep

Examine your friends and the company that you keep. Ask yourself, "Are my friends helping or hindering my process of recovery?" If they are wanting to pull you back, it is time to reassess and find a new circle of friends, ones who can support your new way of being.

The creator has given you free will. What you do with it is up to you. You have the freedom to avoid people, places and circumstances that might contribute to your negative habits.

5. Get professional help

Many recovering addicts have found the counseling provided through a professional therapist, a support group or a 12-Step program to be essential in overcoming their addiction.

There are many different programs and approaches to treatment. Some people do well with 12-Step programs. Some do well with programs focused on mindfulness. Find one that fits your needs and that you feel confident about. Ask your Higher Self and the ascended master Kuthumi to help you find the right program and the right people to help you.

6. Serve others

One of the patterns of addiction is focusing on our own problems. They loom so large that we don't see any way out, and the addiction is a temporary reprieve.

Serving others helps to gain a more objective and realistic perspective. We find that other people have problems, just as we do. We also see that there is a way out.

Service to others also gives a new focus to life. Instead of our addiction being the central organizing principle, we can make a new life centered on serving others.

7. Keep going

Every addict knows about the ups and downs of recovery—Now I'm free! Now I'm not! The ride through addiction and recovery is often a rollercoaster of emotions—fear and elation, pride and shame, hope and disappointment, guilt and acceptance. The sense of hopelessness can be overwhelming, the feeling that "I can never rise above this. I can never master my life."

Sometimes there is nothing that can replace stubborn persistence. Daniel certainly had it. No matter what is happening in your life, remember that history is full of people who have overcome all odds. By the grace of God you can be one of them.

You can do anything with God's help.

No matter how low you get, keep getting up.

You can do anything that you want to do.

God in you can do it!

WHERE TO GET HELP

The following are a few of the many resources available for help in overcoming addiction.

Programs for Addiction
Alcoholics Anonymous
www.aa.org

Narcotics Anonymous
www.na.org

Gamblers Anonymous
www.gamblersanonymous.org

Twelve-Step programs for many other addictions can be found using a web search.

Adult Children of Alcoholics
A 12-Step program for those who grew up in alcoholic, abusive or otherwise dysfunctional families
www.adultchildren.org

Online resources and forums for those seeking to overcome pornography addiction
www.yourbrainonporn.com

National database of behavioral health treatment facilities maintained by the Substance Abuse and Mental Health Services Administration
findtreatment.samhsa.gov

National directory of addiction treatment centers and support groups (AA, etc.)
www.addiction.com

Spiritual Techniques
For more information about the science of the spoken Word and other spiritual techniques to address addiction, contact The Summit Lighthouse.
www.SummitLighthouse.org

Diet
Nutrition in Recovery
www.nutritioninrecovery.com

Center for Addiction Nutrition
www.centerforaddictionnutrition.com

Exercise
Phoenix Multisport
phoenixmultisport.org

Search the Internet for other local sport and fitness clubs.

Yoga
Yoga programs are available in every city, including many that are free. There are many videos online that teach basic postures. Search on YouTube or go to www.doyogawithme.com

Meditation and Mindfulness
www.addictionrecoveryguide.org/holistic/meditation_spirituality

A free app with an easy-to-learn meditation technique is available for Apple and Android phones from 1 Giant Mind.
www.1giantmind.org

Thomas and Beverley Bien, *Mindful Recovery: A Spiritual Path to Healing from Addiction* (New York: Wiley, 2002)

Darren Littlejohn, *The 12-Step Buddhist—Enhance Recovery from Any Addiction* (New York: Atria Books, 2009)

NOTES

PART 1

Prayer and fasting. Matt. 17:21.

PART 2

Ninety percent of people addicted to nicotine. "Tobacco Facts and Figures" at https://betobaccofree.hhs.gov/about-tobacco/facts-figures/

One in three people who commit suicide are under the influence of drugs or alcohol. Carolyn C. Ross, "Suicide: One of Addiction's Hidden Risks," *Psychology Today* blog, posted February 20, 2014. psychologytoday.com

Sources for statistics on addiction:

http://www.theguardian.com/news/datablog/interactive/2012/jul/02/drug -use-map-world

http://www.treatmentsolutions.com/worldwide-drug-statistics/

Rachel N. Lipari et al., "America's Need for and Receipt of Substance Use Treatment in 2015," *The CBHSQ Report,* September 29, 2016. https://www.samhsa.gov/data/sites/default/files/report_2716/ShortReport -2716.pdf

http://www.interceptinterventions.com/resources/facts-and-statistics-about-addiction/

Three to four percent of the population have a gambling problem. National Council on Problem Gambling. http://www.ncpgambling.org/help-treatment/faq/

Kinsey Institute survey. See Kirsten Weir, "Is Pornography Addictive?" *Monitor on Psychology,* vol. 45, no. 4, April 2014, page 46. Online at http://www.apa.org/monitor/2014/04/pornography.aspx. Accessed 11/6/2016.

Increased rates of sexual problems in young men. For a survey of academic studies on this subject, see http://www.yourbrainonporn.com/research-confirms-sharp-rise-youthful-ed

His craving for alcohol. C.G. Jung to William G. Wilson, January 30, 1961.

PART 3

If we were to live, we had to be free of anger. *Alcoholics Anonymous: The Big Book,* 4th ed. (Alcoholics Anonymous World Services, 2012), p. 66.

The dammed-up emotions of years. Ibid., p.62

I now discover how wonderful I am. Louise L. Hay, *You Can Heal Your Life* (Hay House, 1984), back cover, p. 176.

A genetic component to addiction. National institute on Alcohol Abuse and Addiction, "A Family History of Alcoholism: Are You at Risk?" NIH Publication No. 03-5304 (2012).

PART 5

Sources of the material in Part 5:

Mark L. Prophet and Elizabeth Clare Prophet, *The Path to* Immortality (Gardiner, Mont.: Summit University Press, 2006), chapter 4, "Entities."

Elizabeth Clare Prophet, "The Attack on Youth: Drugs, Alcohol, Nicotine and Sugar," part A, October 6, 1977.

Saint Germain, "The Ancient Story of the Drug Conspiracy," *Pearls of Wisdom*, vol. 27, no. 32, June 10, 1984.

Resist the devil. James 4:7.

Persistence of marijuana in the body and brain. Hardin B. Jones and Helen C. Jones, *Sensual Drugs: Deprivation and Rehabilitation of the Mind* (Cambridge: Cambridge University Press, 1977), pp. 303–07.

Marijuana use and schizophrenia. For links to these studies and many more, see http://www.schizophrenia.com/prevention/streetdrugs.html

"Pot Smoking in America," *The Coming Revolution*, Spring 1986.

Fallen angels in physical bodies. See Elizabeth Clare Prophet, *Fallen Angels and the Origins of Evil* (Gardiner, Mont.: Summit University Press, 2000).

PART 6

The light which lighteth every man. John 1:9.

Now are we the sons of God. 1 John 3:2.

Saint Germain, "May You Pass Every Test," in Mark L. Prophet and Elizabeth Clare Prophet, *Lords of the Seven Rays*, Book 2, Chapter 7.

The name of God. Exod. 3:13–15.

A fire round about. Zech. 2:5.

The transfiguration. Luke 9:29.

PART 7

David Wiss on deficiencies in addicts. Jeanene Swanson, "Nutrition for Addicts: Healing the Body," posted July 8, 2014. https://www.addiction.com /3446/nutrition-for-addicts/

We commonly see B vitamin deficiencies. Ibid.

Victoria Abel, "Nourish the Addict's Body," article from Center for Addiction Nutrition website. www.centerforaddictionnutrition.com

James Fell, "Exercise: Alternative Reward for Those Battling Addiction," *Chicago Tribune*, June 12, 2013. www.chicagotribune.com

Fifty percent reduction in drug use through exercise. In this article, Fell reports on a 2011 study at Vanderbilt University of marijuana users. After just a few sessions of 30 minutes running on a treadmill, participants reported a dramatic drop in cravings and a decrease of more than 50% in their drug use. These were people who were considered marijuana dependent and didn't even want to give up—exercise alone changed their behavior. Fell also quotes a study showing that exercise reduced the use of many other drugs, including cocaine, meth, nicotine and alcohol.

Jennifer Matesa, "How Exercise Keeps You Sober," January 16, 2012. www.thefix.com

Stacie Stukin, "Yoga for Addiction Recovery," *Yoga Journal,* October 11, 2012.

Benefits of yoga. A web search for "yoga and addiction" will lead to many articles about the benefits of yoga for those in recovery.

Benefits of meditation in dealing with stress. Even the military is studying the benefits of meditation. In one study, researchers observed two groups of Marines preparing for deployment. One group spent two hours a week for eight weeks practicing mindfulness meditation, a second group did not meditate. Those who meditated showed improved mood and memory, and they were able to stay alert and function more effectively in the high-stress situations of combat. See Amishi P. Jha et al., "Examining the Protective Effects of Mindfulness Training on Working Memory Capacity and Affective Experience," *Emotion,* vol. 10, no. 1, Feb 2010, pp. 54–64. http://dx.doi.org/10.1037/a0018438

If you journal about a relapse. Thomas Beverley Bien, *Mindful Recovery: A Spiritual Path to Healing from Addiction* (New York: Wiley, 2002), p. 81.

Every once in a while. Ibid., p. 85.

Your journal is the friend. Ibid., p. 88.

We need ways to be present with life. Ibid., p. 91.

Videos of nature in prisons. Terrence McCoy, "The stunningly simple idea that could change solitary confinement as we know it," *Washington Post,* October 12, 2015.

Healing effects of nature. Frederick Reimers, "Nature Rx," *Outside,* November 2016, pp. 46–48.

Vengeance is mine. Rom. 12:19.

Stanton Peele, *Recover! An Empowering Program to Help You Stop Thinking Like an Addict and Reclaim Your Life* (Boston: Da Capo Press, 2015), p. 15.

PART 8

Darren Littlejohn, *The 12-Step Buddhist—Enhance Recovery from Any Addiction* (New York: Atria Books, 2009), p. xvi.

Third-Step Prayer. *Alcoholics Anonymous: The Big Book* (2001), p. 63.

Seventh-Step Prayer. Ibid., p. 76.

PART 9

Sins of the fathers. Exod. 20:5, 34:7; Deut. 5:9; Num. 14:18.

Remember their sins no more. Heb. 8:12.

The danger of allowing entities to come back. Matt. 12:42–44.